TRIVIA
BOOK

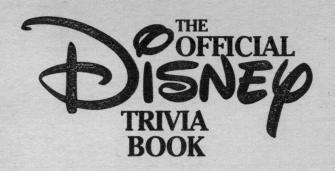

THE OFFICIAL DISNEY TRIVIA BOOK

**Bill Ginch
and
Fred Miranda**

PaperJacks LTD.

TORONTO   NEW YORK

PaperJacks LTD

TORONTO   NEW YORK

THE OFFICIAL DISNEY TRIVIA BOOK

PaperJacks Ltd.

330 Steelcase Rd. E., Markham, Ont. L3R 2M1
210 Fifth Ave., New York, N.Y. 10010

Paperjacks edition published December 1988

All photos courtesy of The Walt Disney Company

10 9 8 7 6 5 4 3 2 1

ISBN 07701-1002-9

Printed in the USA

To my wife, Debbie, and my son, Michael, who are my life and breath. The joys and mysteries of one's life would be but one-dimensional with no one to share them with. I have been truly blessed with these two amazing people, who make each day a loving experience and each accomplishment a celebration of growth and learning. My love for them is endless, as is my gratitude for their patience.

—F.M.

To my wife, Laurie, a dream come true. Walt Disney always said, "If you wish long and hard enough, that wish will come true." He was so right. I thank her for all her love and support, which she gives so freely and unconditionally. She adds a new meaning to the word happiness. How lucky I am to have her as my wife.

—B.G.

Acknowledgments

We wish to thank the folks at Disney Studios for their assistance in compiling the information contained in this book:

Photo Library
Barbara Gunderson   Joanne Warren

Archives

Dave Smith
Karen Brower   Paula Sigman   Rose Motzko

Publications

Karen Kreider

Special thanks to Robyn Tynan of the Publications Department, whose help was instrumental in completing this work. We cannot express how much we appreciate her direction and assistance with this project.

Contents

Introduction

Since childhood, like many of you, we have been fascinated by Walt Disney. Those two words didn't so much represent a man or a production company, but rather a feeling. As a matter of fact, it came as quite a shock to learn that Walt Disney was a man. The joy and happiness that he bestowed upon us was usually associated with the likes of Santa Claus and other fictitious, larger-than-life characters. How could one man, we asked ourselves over and over, be responsible for thoroughly entertaining so many people?

We can all recall our first encounters with the Disney mystique without too much trouble. Impressive television and print campaigns everywhere let us know what was coming next from the master himself. You never had to ask Mom and Dad twice to take you to a Disney feature film; they were all too happy to accompany you. A Walt Disney film never left you disappointed. You traveled home from the theater on a cloud. The film was only the beginning for poor Mom and Dad, who would have to buy the books, puzzles, and records based on the film, such was our desire to relive the movie many times over. Those were the days; life was terrific and Disney was Disney. For both of us, the main reason we got our homework done so quickly each night was so we could have it out of the way in time to devote all our attention to "The Mickey Mouse Club." We each carried our Honorary Mouseketeer Club Membership Cards proudly, gladly showing them to anyone who asked and many who didn't. Who would have thought that many years later we would have the chance to research the very shows we watched each evening while wearing our Official Mouseketeer Ears?

For a number of years it has been our wish to pay tribute to the greatness of Walt Disney, the man and the institution. The problem was how to do this. Biographies have been written and documentaries have been filmed. We finally agreed that the most fun way to honor Walt Disney was simply to present some of his work through trivia questions. We also agreed that by presenting these works in this manner we could focus on the attention to detail for which Disney became so famous. This book will involve you totally in the magic of Walt Disney and recreate those classic moments in entertainment for which he is beloved.

While doing research for this book we not only learned a great deal about Disney's actual films, but also about the effect Walt Disney has had on the lives of others. It was at the Disney Studios in Burbank, California, that we were best able to put Walt Disney's accomplishments into perspective. His presence is felt or seen at every turn. The fact, for example, that every office in the Animation Building, no matter how small, has a window, is the direct result of Walt's insistence that the beautiful California weather could serve as a refresher for his hard-working staff. He always wanted his employees to feel at home, and it's clear that goal has been accomplished. Today The Walt Disney Company employs more than 30,000 people worldwide, with probably close to 1,000,000 applications on file. The real tribute to Walt Disney, then, is not in any scrapbook chock-full of glowing film reviews or in a showcase housing his countless awards, or even in a trivia teaser like this. The real tribute is on the face of every one of his employees at the Disney Studios, at

Disneyland, or at EPCOT Center. His spirit lives in these places. Not just lives ... thrives.

Our book is divided into four main sections, each representing the diversity of Disney. There are trivia questions on the classic animated Disney films, as well as a variety of live-action Disney full-length features. There is also a section devoted to Walt Disney's impact on television. Finally, there are quizzes on the most ambitious of Walt Disney's dreams—the theme parks: Disneyland, Walt Disney World, and EPCOT Center.

In the initial section, we have included questions on twenty of Disney's animated classics. The animated film is perhaps what Walt Disney is best known for, and viewing these films explains why. Few others have come close to the level of excellence in entertainment the films demonstrate.

The questions based on Disney's TV productions zero in on the popular "Mickey Mouse Club" and the long-running "Wonderful World of Disney" series. Year after year, Tinker Bell would summon us to our television sets, and we were bereft when she no longer brought Disney, in living color, into our living rooms. Fans should note that for the new season, Disney has scheduled brand-new episodes of "Davy Crockett," a program that has become a cult classic since its initial run on TV.

The section devoted to Disney's live-action films contains many of the best-known Disney productions, as well as some of our personal favorites. The Disney name is synonymous with family entertainment, in fact. For many years, Walt Disney Productions was the only major studio regularly producing family entertainment films. Walt Disney's untimely death left the world in a state of disbelief, and many wondered if the family film would die with him. His ideas continue to be carried out by the dedicated people at The Walt Disney Studios.

Finally, on your trivia journey, you will visit the Walt Disney theme parks. We hope these questions give you a sense of the vastness of these projects. Once you have realized what an impossible dream the parks were, you will be closer to understanding the genius of the man who made the impossible happen.

We are sure this book will stir memories within you that have been dormant too long. It will most assuredly bring a smile to your face, and that, in itself, is perhaps the most appropriate tribute to Walt Disney.

DISNEY'S
ANIMATED
CLASSICS

The animated film is, without question, the most enchanting of all the fields of entertainment Disney has mastered. It is in a class by itself, and, wisely, few have ventured to copy it. Walt Disney gathered around him a team of the most creative artists, animators, and storytellers he could find, and under his leadership, they created the Disney animated classics we cherish today. Chief among his animators was the group he affectionately referred to as his "nine old men" (in spite of the fact they were all young at the time). They were Les Clark, Marc Davis, Ollie Johnston, Milt Kahl, Ward Kimball, Eric Larson, John Lounsbery, Frank Thomas, and Woolie Reitherman. The skills of these animators and their colleagues translated into the Disney magic we see on our local theater screens.

Walt Disney never stopped developing new and remarkable animation techniques, but hard work and imagination were the most effective "techniques" of all. To him there was always a way to make a film better. The only thing that stopped him from continually striving to perfect what he'd already done was his fascination with the next project he had planned. And there was always another project.

Snow White
and the Seven Dwarfs

Released: December 1937
Running Time: 83 Minutes

Snow White was the first full-length animated film to be produced. This extravaganza is the culmination of the work of 750 artists, including 32 animators, 102 assistants, 20 layout artists, 25 background artists, 65 special-effects artists, 158 ink and paint artists, and countless others. This film set the tone for the remarkable things that Walt Disney would create for many years to follow and in 1939, was honored with a special Academy Award for pioneering "a great new entertainment field for the motion picture cartoon."

Now don't be bashful. We're quite sure you'll come up with the right answers to the trivia questions that follow.

QUESTIONS

SNOW WHITE AND THE SEVEN DWARFS

1. At the beginning of the film, we see Snow White singing as the handsome prince joins her. What song is she singing?

2. The wicked queen calls upon a huntsman to bring her the heart of Snow White. Of course, we all know he does not carry through with the order, even though he does deliver a heart to the queen. From where does that heart come?

3. When do we first encounter the Seven Dwarfs?

4. For what marching song are the Seven Dwarfs famous?

5. Who tells the dwarfs that Snow White is in danger?

6. Who helps Snow White clean the dwarfs' cottage, and what song does she sing?

7. With what is the wicked queen obsessed?

8. Can you name all Seven Dwarfs?

9. Who provided the voice of Snow White?

10. Who is the only dwarf not to have a beard?

11. How many teeth does Dopey have?

12. What is Grumpy's first opinion of Snow White?

13. According to the film, what is the only thing that can save Snow White after she bites into the poisoned apple?

14. Which one of the Seven Dwarfs is considered the group's leader?

15. What are the six ingredients the queen uses to turn herself into an old hag?

16. The role of the prince is considered to be crucial, but we see him only for two short scenes. What are they?

17. What was so unusual about the Academy Award Walt Disney won for *Snow White and the Seven Dwarfs?*

18. What kind of pie is Snow White making for the Seven Dwarfs when she is visited by the wicked queen transformed into an old hag?

19. How does the wicked witch entice Snow White into eating the poisoned apple?

20. What two things make up the coffin built by the Seven Dwarfs for Snow White?

Answers on p. 181

Pinocchio

Released: February 1940
Running Time: 88 Minutes

Two years were spent creating Walt Disney Studios'
version of *Pinocchio,* which was released in 1940 by
RKO Radio Pictures in Technicolor. More than 450,000
drawings and paintings were used to weave the magic
we eventually beheld on the big screen. Many critics
feel this is the most elaborate, and perhaps most beautiful of Walt Disney's animated films.

Answer the "no strings attached" questions based on this Disney classic and help bring our little hero to life once again.

QUESTIONS

PINOCCHIO

1. Who wrote the story of a little puppet who dreamed of being a real boy?

2. What is the name of the Oscar-winning song sung by Jiminy Cricket?

3. What is the name of the wood carver who made Pinocchio?

4. What are the names of the wood carver's kitten and fish?

5. What is the name of the whale in *Pinocchio*?

6. What happens to Pinocchio whenever he tells a lie?

7. What object carried by Jiminy Cricket was also carried by Mary Poppins?

8. What does Geppetto notice while looking out the window before going to bed?

9. What is Geppetto's wish, and who grants it?

10. Of what is Pinocchio made?

11. According to the Blue Fairy, Pinocchio has to do three things, in order, to become a real boy. What are they?

12. What "role" does Jiminy Cricket play in Pinocchio's life?

13. According to a song, what does Jiminy Cricket tell Pinocchio to do if he "gets in trouble and he doesn't know what to do"?

14. In what does Jiminy Cricket sleep at Geppetto's?

15. For what type of show is Stromboli famous?

16. Who sells Pinocchio to Stromboli, and where does he keep Pinocchio?

17. Who sings "Hi-Diddle-Dee-Dee (An Actor's Life for Me)"?

18. What is the name of the place from which boys never return as boys?

19. What happens to boys on Pleasure Island?

20. What does Pinocchio eat on Pleasure Island?

21. How does Pinocchio learn about Geppetto's fate?

22. How do Pinocchio and Geppetto escape from Monstro?

23. Who turns Pinocchio into a real boy?

24. What gift does the Blue Fairy give Jiminy Cricket?

25. Who saves Geppetto from drowning?

Answers on p. 182

FANTASIA

Released: November 1940
Running Time: 120 Minutes

What made this film remarkable was Disney's interpretation of the music incorporated within. The film represented a combination of the world's most beautiful musical compositions and the genius of Walt Disney. Only Disney's innovative animation could do justice to such marvelous music. Interestingly, when *Fantasia* was released in 1940, many critics said that audiences weren't ready for it, that it was 30 years ahead of its time. They were right: Twenty-nine years later it was re-released to overwhelming admiration, and it has continued to delight audiences ever since.

Please conduct yourselves well as you orchestrate the answers to the questions that follow.

QUESTIONS

FANTASIA

1. What is unique about the soundtrack of this film classic?

2. Who conducted the orchestra in this Disney spectacular?

3. In the opening segment, "Toccata and Fugue in D Minor," what is the first thing the viewer sees?

4. Which instrumentalists are featured prominently in this scene?

5. In the next sequence, "The Nutcracker Suite," six movements of the classic composition are featured. In one movement, "Dance of the Sugar Plum Fairies," what type of fairies do the dancing?

6. "Chinese Dance" features what type of dancing vegetable? What is the name of the smallest dancer, who can't seem to keep in step?

7. How is "The Dance of the Reed Flutes" represented in animated wonder?

8. Where does the "Arabian Dance" sequence take place?

9. Thistles resembling Cossacks do the footwork in this next-to-last dance sequence. What is it called?

10. In "The Waltz of the Flowers," three types of seasonal fairies do the dancing. Can you name them?

11. What famous Disney character appears in "The Sorcerer's Apprentice"?

12. What item does the Sorcerer's Apprentice "borrow" in order to perform magic?

13. What act of magic gets our cute little star in a great deal of trouble in this scene?

14. What scientific theory is represented in the next segment, which features Igor Stravinsky's "Rite of Spring?"

15. What is the audience treated to, visually, in the opening sequence, entitled "Trip Through Space"?

16. In "Rite of Spring" what two species of dinosaur are locked in mortal combat?

17. In what country and time is "The Pastoral Symphony" set?

18. In the opening sequence of "The Pastoral Symphony," entitled "Mount Olympus," what mythological flying creature is featured?

19. In the third movement, "Bacchanal," what is the name of Bacchus's donkey-unicorn?

20. Who hurls lighting bolts at Bacchus in the movement entitled "The Storm"?

21. "The Dance of the Hours" features four animal ballets. Can you recall the four types of animals featured in this segment?

22. The film's finale is Mussorgsky's "Night on Bald Mountain" and "Ave Maria." Where can one find Bald Mountain?

23. On what night do all the ghosts and evil spirits gather on Bald Mountain?

24. What is the name of the Devil?

25. Bells, signaling the coming of morning, drive all the ghosts and evil spirits back from whence they came. But the bells also serve another purpose. What is that purpose?

Answers on p. 184

DUMBO

Released: October 1941
Running Time: 63½ Minutes

Walt Disney's *Dumbo* has the shortest running time of any of the animated classics produced by Disney Studios. The story, by Helen Aberson and Harold Pearl, was transformed into a motion picture in just a year and a half by Walt Disney, making it one of the least expensive of the animated classics to produce. The lead character of the film remains, to this day, one of the most beloved and recognizable of all Disney creations in spite of the fact he never speaks a word.

Although short on time, this film is long on happy memories, many of which you will recall as you attempt to answer correctly the questions that follow.

QUESTIONS

DUMBO

1. What is the name of Dumbo's mother?

2. In the beginning of the film, we see that many of the circus animals are expecting little bundles of joy. In fact, the animals are all waiting for their new ones at the winter quarters of the circus. In what state are the winter quarters located?

3. How does Dumbo first reveal his large floppy ears?

4. Dumbo's mother is riding the train who "thinks he can" when the stork finally delivers her bundle of joy. What is the train's name?

5. Dumbo is delivered by the messenger stork. Who was the voice of the stork? (Hint: He later became the voice of Winnie the Pooh.)

6. What name does Dumbo receive from his mother?

7. Who gives Dumbo his more popular name?

8. Since the other elephants want no part of Dumbo, he is befriended by a little mouse. Can you tell us the mouse's name?

9. Why does the pyramid of elephants collapse?

10. After his first attempt at becoming a star proves disastrous, Dumbo is forced to work as part of the clown act. What is the "joke" the clowns play on him?

11. After this joke, the clowns get drunk and sing a song. What is the name of this song?

12. At one point, Dumbo and Timothy get drunk and Dumbo begins to hallucinate. What did he imagine, that later became a classic scene in animation?

13. The five crows give Dumbo a "magic talisman" to help him fly. What do they give him?

14. What is the name of the classic song sung by the five crows?

15. At the end of the film, for how much are Dumbo's ears insured?

Answers on p. 186

Bambi

Released: August 1942
Running Time: 69½ Minutes

In order to ensure that the animals' movements in this animated classic were authentic, the state of Maine sent Walt Disney two fawns for his artists to use as live models. Accordingly, Bambi and his mate in the film were patterned after those fawns. Another unique thing about this film is that there are fewer than a thousand words spoken throughout. The visual effects are so exceptional that even that much dialogue seems unnecessary.

So gather all your forest friends as you try to answer the following questions.

QUESTIONS

BAMBI

1. Who brings the news to the animals of the forest that Bambi, a new prince, has been born?

2. Who helps Bambi learn to speak?

3. When Bambi encounters a skunk for the first time, what does he call him?

4. What is the name of Bambi's true love?

5. How do the animals refer to Bambi's father?

6. What winter sport does Thumper teach Bambi when the temperatures reach freezing?

7. How does Bambi's mother die?

8. What is the name of the owl that advises many of the forest animals?

9. Who wants to fight Bambi in order to decide which of them gets Faline?

10. Later in the film, Bambi saves the life of the doe he loves. From whom does he save her?

11. How is Bambi wounded in the film?

12. What is the little doe's mother's name?

13. How many "children" does Bambi's mate give birth to in the film?

14. When Bambi asks what caused the terror and commotion in the forest that sent all the animals into a frenzy, his father answers with five telling words. Do you recall his response?

15. What word does the owl use to describe the feeling in spring that young animals get when they begin to discover the opposite sex?

16. In this film, Bambi becomes fast and close friends with a rabbit. What is this rabbit's mother's name?

17. What title has Bambi gained by film's end?

18. What is Bambi's first word?

Answers on p. 187

Song of the South

Released: November 1946
Running Time: 94 Minutes

Song of the South was the first Disney film to have a completely human cast, although it also incorporated the magic of animated characters in several memorable scenes. With the tales of Uncle Remus presented in full animation, this film featured all variations of live action–animated film techniques and will always be considered a groundbreaking classic. The actor portraying Uncle Remus received a special Academy Award for his heartwarming characterization of the beloved storyteller.

Enjoy the feeling of all that fresh country air and that remarkable country hospitality as you swing on the back porch and try to come up with the correct answers to these questions.

QUESTIONS

SONG OF THE SOUTH

1. Who plays the role of Uncle Remus in this fascinating Disney offering?

2. Johnny comes to stay with his grandmother (where he meets Uncle Remus) because his father is away on business. What is his father's profession?

3. Why does Johnny want to run away from his grandmother's house?

4. What song from this film won an Academy Award, and who wrote it?

5. Who plays the role of Johnny's mother in this film?

6. To dissuade Johnny from running away, Uncle Remus tells him what happened to Brer Rabbit when he attempted to run away from the briar patch. What happened?

7. How does Brer Rabbit escape this tricky situation?

8. Who is Brer Rabbit's main antagonist in all the tales told by Uncle Remus?

9. According to Uncle Remus, why can't you run away from trouble?

10. Who gives Johnny the puppy that triggers the problem of ownership and, in turn, the next tale by Uncle Remus?

11. Who lies and says Johnny stole the puppy?

12. To prove a point to Johnny, Uncle Remus tells a story about the Tar Baby. In the story, which animals greet Brer Rabbit as he strolls through the woods?

13. Why is Brer Rabbit offended by the creature made of tar?

14. How is this Tar Baby, in reality, a trap set for Brer Rabbit?

15. The next humorous tale is triggered after Johnny and Ginny have been harassed by her brothers. What is its title?

16. Where does Brer Rabbit lead his captors in order to escape becoming their next meal?

17. What type of animated bird appears in the final sequence of this film?

18. In that final scene, Uncle Remus is seen singing with Johnny and Ginny. One other little boy joined them. Can you remember his name?

19. Who wrote the Uncle Remus stories, on which parts of this film are based?

20. What is unusual about the actor who provided the voice for Brer Fox in this film?

Answers on p. 188

Cinderella

Released: February 1950
Running Time: 74 Minutes

Research done by Walt Disney while attempting to bring this beloved tale to the screen in animated form revealed surprising information about the famous glass slipper: it wasn't meant to be glass at all! In fact, it was originally supposed to have been made of fur (*pantouffle en vair*), which, by mistake, became glass when the story by Charles Perrault was translated from the French.

We don't want you to feel any pressure, but if you want to avoid that whole pumpkin routine, we'd suggest you answer these questions before the clock strikes twelve.

QUESTIONS

CINDERELLA

1. Who was the voice of Cinderella?

2. What is the name of the only animal hostile to Cinderella?

3. What is the name of Cinderella's wicked stepmother?

4. After her father dies, how does the Stepmother treat Cinderella?

5. What are the names of Cinderella's two stepsisters?

6. Mice figure prominently in this film. What are the names of the two most notable ones?

7. Which of these two mice is rescued by Cinderella from a mousetrap?

8. Why does the king instruct his grand duke to organize a ball?

9. According to the king, who will be invited to the ball?

10. Cinderella's stepmother allows her to go to the ball if she can accomplish what two things?

11. What instrument does Cinderella's stepmother play?

12. What is the name of Cinderella's fairy godmother?

13. What color is the fairy godmother's outfit?

14. The fairy godmother uses what three magical words to make her magic work?

15. What does the fairy godmother use to make a coach?

16. What animals are turned into a coachman, footman, and the white horses?

17. As the fairy godmother said, "Dreams can't last forever." At what time, according to the fairy godmother, does the magic spell expire?

18. What song do Cinderella and Prince Charming sing as they are dancing at the ball?

19. What are the slippers made of that Cinderella wears to the ball?

20. What three characters help Cinderella escape from her tower room at the end of the film?

Answers on p. 190

ALICE in WONDERLAND

Released: July 1951
Running Time: 75 Minutes

Bringing this classic tale to the big screen in animated form without losing the sense of fantasy that makes it so mesmerizing would appear to be a tremendous undertaking. Walt Disney made it look easy. It lost none of its charm and, in fact, Disney's animation made the adventure even more exciting with the use of exaggerated characters and brilliant colors. The music from the film is at least as distinctive as the film itself; at the time of the film's release, 10 of its songs were available in close to 40 variations, some recorded by as many as 6 artists.

Check your pocket watches so you won't be late in answering the following questions.

QUESTIONS

ALICE IN WONDERLAND

1. As the film opens, we find Alice in a tree listening to someone read her a history lesson. Who is reading to Alice?

2. What is the name of Alice's kitten, as revealed in the opening scene?

3. Where is Alice looking when she sees a fantastic creature and her adventure begins?

4. Who does Alice see that leads her into Wonderland? (Hint: Chasing this character forms the basis for her entire adventure.)

5. When Alice's journey is interrupted because she can't fit through a certain door, who advises her to drink a magic potion that will make her shrink?

6. When Alice drinks the potion, she describes its taste. With each of the four sips she takes, she changes her mind. How many of the four flavors that Alice mentions can you name?

7. Alice does in fact shrink, but has left the key to the door on a table she can now no longer reach. How does Alice eventually get through the door?

8. Upon passing through the door, with what character does Alice come in contact?

9. When Alice's chase begins again, she is drawn into a forest. What two twin characters does she meet?

10. What story is told to Alice by the two characters she has met in the forest?

11. In this Curiosity-Killed-the-Cat-type story that Alice is told as a warning to discontinue her chase, what type of creatures are done in by their curiosity?

12. When Alice finally catches up with the character she has been pursuing so ardently, he calls her by a different name. What is it?

13. Alice eats another wafer and grows to an enormous size, bursting out of the roof and windows of the White Rabbit's house. What do the characters who see her like this call her?

14. Whose services are enlisted to rid the house of the now larger-than-life Alice?

15. What food does Alice eat in order to shrink?

16. Alice wanders again into the forest and encounters several insects. What is unusual about these insects?

17. Alice meets up with a group of talking flowers. What song do the talking flowers sing for Alice?

18. When the flowers cannot recognize her species and reject her as one of their own, what do they assume Alice is?

19. Alice then meets an insect who blows "smoke-ring" letters. What type of insect is he?

20. Alice is shown a vegetable and told that eating one side will make her grow, while eating the other side will have the reverse effect. What type of vegetable is this?

21. Upon continuing her journey, Alice meets up with a character perched in a tree who will cause her great problems for the remainder of her adventure. Whom does Alice meet?

22. Upon asking where she can find the character she has been chasing, Alice is referred to the Mad Hatter and the March Hare for guidance. What song are they singing when Alice comes upon them?

23. The Mad Hatter has a card attached to his hat. What is written on the card?

24. When Alice mentions her cat, a little dormouse goes into hysterics. How is Alice advised to calm him down by the Mad Hatter and the March Hare?

25. What nonsensical riddle does the Mad Hatter ask Alice?

26. Alice stumbles upon a sign that directs her into the woods. What is the name of the wood, as stated on this sign?

27. Who then shows Alice a shortcut to meet the Queen of Hearts?

28. Who are the first characters Alice encounters on her journey to meet the queen?

29. The Queen of Hearts, whom Alice had desperately wanted to meet, isn't as friendly as Alice hoped. In fact, the queen has Alice put on trial for teasing, tormenting, and generally annoying her. What is Alice's sentence?

30. Who provided the voices for the following characters?

    a. Alice
    b. Cheshire Cat
    c. Mad Hatter
    d. March Hare

Answers on p. 191

Peter Pan

Released: February 1953
Running Time: 76½ Minutes

Peter Pan, at the time of its release, was Walt Disney's most ambitious venture. It took more than a decade of preparation, three years of production, and cost more than $3,000,000. For the first time, all the main characters are human or have human characteristics, as is the case with Tinker Bell and the mermaids. Its fantasy perhaps personifies Disney's film magic better than any of the other animated classics.

Walt Disney takes us on a voyage to a land beyond our imagination that we will never forget. Answering the following questions will once again prepare you for that journey and keep you young forever!

QUESTIONS

PETER PAN

1. *Peter Pan* is based on the work of what well-known writer?

2. For what does Peter Pan search as the story begins?

3. In what great city does the story begin?

4. In the opening of the film, we are introduced to the Darling family. Give us the first names of Mr. and Mrs. Darling, and tell us what Mrs. Darling thought Peter Pan was.

5. How many children do the Darlings have, and what are their names?

6. Who is Peter Pan's tiny companion, and what kind of creature is she?

7. The Darling children have a nursemaid. What is her name, and what is so unusual about her?

8. What is Never Land?

9. How does one get to Never Land?

10. According to Peter Pan, where is Never Land located?

11. Who is the pirate captain always chasing Peter Pan?

12. Name the captain's sidekick, who always makes things seem worse than they really are?

13. How did the captain get his name?

14. Why is there an crocodile always chasing the captain?

15. How does the captain know when the crocodile is near him?

16. Who is the Indian chief's daughter who gets kidnapped by the evil captain?

17. Where does the captain take her after kidnapping her?

18. What is the entrance to Peter Pan's hiding place?

19. What is Peter Pan's nickname for the pirate captain?

20. How do Peter Pan and the children get back to London?

Answers on p. 194

Lady and the Tramp

Released: June 1955
Running Time: 75½ Minutes

This animated classic produced by the Disney Studios has often been referred to as Walt's "happiest motion picture." *Lady and the Tramp* was the first animated feature to use the widescreen format of CinemaScope.

It actually was filmed twice, once in standard format and once for the CinemaScope cameras, which provided a wider stage on which to place the action.

Set primarily in the suburbs of a midsize American city, the film took us into a world that is very much like our own today. The opening scene was actually a rewrite of an event that took place in the life of Walt himself. After a meaningless argument with his wife, Walt thought the best way to make up with her was to surprise her with a puppy—not just any dog, but a cute little cocker spaniel that later on would inspire him to create this feature.

We sincerely hope you do not find the following trivia questions, based on some of Disney's favorite canine characters, too "ruff"!

QUESTIONS

LADY AND THE TRAMP

1. Who wrote the songs for *Lady and the Tramp*?

2. According to the story, what is one thing money can't buy?

3. During what season of the year does the story open and end?

4. What are the names of Lady's owners?

5. What happens to the newspaper when Lady brings it in?

6. How old was Lady when she received her dog license?

7. What is the color of Lady's collar?

8. What is the name of the dog that wears a plaid sweater, and of his companion who seems to have lost his sense of smell?

9. What is Trusty's grandpappy's name?

10. What is the name of Tramp's favorite Italian restaurant?

11. What two words does Jim utter to upset Lady?

12. During what month does Jim Dear's wife have a baby?

13. During her pregnancy, what does Darling send Jim out for one wintry night?

14. Who watches the baby and Lady when Jim Dear and his wife are away?

15. What type of dog is Lady? Tramp?

16. What type of pets does Aunt Sarah bring to Jim's house?

17. What are the names of Aunt Sarah's pets?

18. What purchase does Aunt Sarah make at the pet shop for Lady?

19. Who comes to Lady's rescue when she is being chased by three dogs?

20. Where do Lady and the Tramp go to free Lady of the muzzle, and who takes the muzzle off her?

21. What does the sign read outside the zoo to which Tramp pays no attention?

22. Who is the cook at Tony's, and what do Lady and Tramp eat there?

23. What is Tramp's nickname for Lady?

24. What do the dogs in the pound call Lady?

25. What song does Peg sing in the pound?

26. According to Peg, what is a dog's passport to freedom?

27. How many puppies do Lady and the Tramp have?

28. What kind of puppies do they have?

29. What happens to Trusty when he follows the dog-catcher's van to save Tramp?

30. What does Aunt Sarah send the dogs for Christmas?

Answers on p. 195

Sleeping Beauty

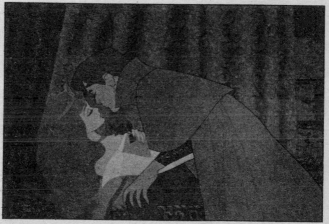

Released: January 1959
Running Time: 75 Minutes

Inspired by Walt Disney's love for Tchaikovsky's *Sleeping Beauty* ballet, this film took six years to complete. It took one million drawings and six million dollars to achieve the tapestry-like 70 mm Technirama spectacular. Disney's guide to the artists who worked on the film was as follows:

> "Make the characters seem as real and believable as life—with all the powers of illusion at your command!"

You might have to summon all your magical powers as well to come up with the correct answers to the following questions.

QUESTIONS

SLEEPING BEAUTY

1. What was the princess's given name when she was born?

2. Why was the princess named after the dawn?

3. What are the names of the three good fairies?

4. Who are King Stefan and King Hubert?

5. Why do Stefan and Hubert arrange their children's marriage?

6. To whom is the princess betrothed?

7. What is the name of the wicked fairy, and what is her gift to the baby princess?

8. According to Fauna, Maleficent knows nothing about what three things in life?

9. In order to protect Aurora, what do the three fairies do?

10. Where does Maleficent live?

11. According to the song, Aurora has lips as red as what flower?

12. Where do the good fairies take Aurora in order to foil Maleficent's prophecy?

13. What "common" name do the fairies give Aurora?

14. Which one of the fairies makes Aurora's birthday cake?

15. What is the name of Prince Phillip's horse?

16. What song do Aurora and Phillip sing in the woods?

17. In what century does *Sleeping Beauty* take place?

18. What do the fairies do to prevent anyone from learning that Aurora has fallen victim to Maleficent's curse?

19. How does the song describe Aurora's hair?

20. What are the weapons of righteousness the fairies give Phillip to fight Maleficent?

21. What type of creature does Maleficent turn into in order to fight Phillip?

22. Into what does Merryweather change Maleficent's raven?

23. What obstacle does Maleficent put around King Stefan's Castle to keep Prince Phillip from reaching the princess?

24. How does Prince Phillip kill the dragon?

Answers on p. 197

101 DALMATIANS

Released: January 1961
Running Time: 79 Minutes

One Hundred and One Dalmatians has been described
as Walt Disney's funniest, most clever animated feature film. It is certainly one of our favorites. A process
called Xerography was adapted for this film, allowing
the animators' drawings to be reproduced exactly onto
cels, and to facilitate the animation of the infinitesimal
number of spots needed for the 101 Dalmatians in the

film. (Nearly 6,500,000 spots figured altogether in this film.) This technique gave *One Hundred and One Dalmatians* a different look from the films that had preceded it.

You'll see spots as you try to answer the following trivia questions on this favorite film. Don't worry, though—after a short "paws" you'll be back to normal.

QUESTIONS

101 DALMATIANS

1. Pongo has the leading-dog role in this excellent Disney film. Who is his owner?

2. Who is Pongo determined to meet and woo, when he sees her out his window?

3. What is the result of the dogs' owners' encounter when Pongo forces a "chance" meeting with his heartthrob?

4. How many puppies are born to Pongo and his mate?

5. Who acts as midwife for the puppies' birth?

6. What evil character offers to buy the puppies, and why does she want them?

7. When her offer is refused, whom does she hire to dognap the puppies?

8. In order to find his kidnapped puppies, Pongo uses a special means of communication to alert the dog and animal community. What is this called?

9. Where have the puppies been hidden?

10. Pongo and his mate attempt to rescue the puppies with the help of three animals. Who are they?

11. How many puppies, in total, have been bought or stolen by Cruella?

12. How do the puppies escape without being recognized by their captor, who is in hot pursuit?

13. After the puppies escape, what two breeds of dogs help them with their long journey home?

14. In what country does this delightful adventure take place?

15. What is unusual about the dogs and their owners seen at the beginning of the film?

16. Which of Perdita's puppies have the most prominent roles in the film? (There are six.)

17. What are the names of the cows who provide the puppies with milk during their long journey home?

18. The Baduns' favorite TV show is a parody of the popular "What's My Line" series. What is this parody called?

19. What character is being questioned on this show?

20. Another TV parody features a superhero collie named Thunderbolt. Who is Thunderbolt's arch enemy?

Answers on p. 198

THE SWORD IN THE STONE

Released: December 1963
Running Time: 79 Minutes

It took nearly three years and 300 artists to create the legendary world of King Arthur for this Disney production. The artists used 1,325,650 pencils to produce more than 1,000,000 separate drawings, which, in turn, were transferred to celluloids through Xerography. "The Sword in the Stone" was the first animated feature to showcase the music of Richard M. Sherman and Robert B. Sherman, two of Disney's most honored staff songwriters.

Your task is a great deal easier than King Arthur's was, since all you must do is think back and answer the following questions.

QUESTIONS

THE SWORD IN THE STONE

1. On which book is this film based, and who wrote it?

2. What is the wizard's name?

3. The wizard has a wise familiar who often gives advice, even when it isn't needed. What kind of animal is he, and what is his most fitting name?

4. The film revolves around a young boy. Can you give his real name, as well as his nickname?

5. Can you name the boy's foster father?

6. How does the boy first meet Merlin?

7. What is so significant about the tournament on New Year's Day?

8. Where is the sword of the title located, and how is it displayed?

9. What is the inscription on the sword?

10. Merlin grants the boy his first wish of becoming something he has always wanted to be. What does the boy wish to become?

11. Merlin turns the boy into two other animals. What are they?

12. What is the name of the female wizard?

13. Who teaches the boy to read and write?

14. How does Madam Mim try to destroy the boy?

15. How do wizards duel?

16. What are the four rules for the Wizard's Duel?

17. How does Merlin win the duel?

18. What is the one thing Madam Mim hates in the whole world?

19. Who eventually pulls the sword from the stone?

20. The young boy learns from Merlin that two important things bestow the real power in life. What are they?

Answers on p. 200

THE JUNGLE BOOK

Released: October 1967
Running Time: 78 Minutes

The Jungle Book, which took three and a half years to make, was the last film with which Walt Disney would have personal "hands on" involvement. It summed up thirty years of ingenious animation techniques.

In addition, the film made use of well-known actors,

as the voices of the characters who were perfectly "married" to their on-screen counterparts. This adds an amazing sense of realism to the film.

The jungle can be a frightening place, so don't go ape as you try to discern the right answers to these questions.

QUESTIONS

THE JUNGLE BOOK

1. Who finds Mowgli, the abandoned man-cub, in the jungle?

2. Mowgli is adopted by wolves. Who is his new "father"?

3. What is the name of the tiger that despises humans and would like nothing better than to capture and devour Mowgli?

4. Who heads the jungle's wolf pack, a tribunal that discusses important jungle issues?

5. What is the name of the hypnotic snake Mowgli encounters on the first night of his journey back to a human village?

6. Who is leader of the elephant herd that Mowgli encounters on his journey?

7. The leader of this herd has his wife with him. What is her name?

8. What is the name of the friendly bear Mowgli meets and becomes instant friends with?

9. Why does Mowgli's panther guardian disapprove of this friendship?

10. What types of animals capture Mowgli?

11. Mowgli is taken by his captors to a temple in the jungle. Who is the leader of this temple and its followers?

12. What "secret" does the king insist Mowgli teach him?

13. Why does the king want to learn this secret? (Hint: the answer is in a song.)

14. When Mowgli escapes from the ape temple, he rebels against the idea of returning to a man-village once again and runs off. Whose help does Bagheera seek to find the boy?

15. What are the names of the four vultures Mowgli meets?

16. How does Mowgli's bear friend supposedly die?

17. Of what is Shere Khan terrified?

18. Why does Mowgli finally agree to return to the man-village?

19. What words of advice does Baloo give Mowgli regarding the opposite sex?

20. What song is performed by the cast as the film ends?

Answers on p. 201

ARISTOCATS

Released: December 1970
Running Time: 78 Minutes

For a single-character scene, each minute of Disney animation requires more than 1,400 drawings. For scenes with more than one character, this number rises considerably. *The Aristocats* was a remarkable feat of animation. Made up of more than 108,000 individual frames, it employed almost 37 miles of film (including pencil tests of several sequences). The film cost more than $4,000,000 to make and took the better part of four years to complete. Famed entertainer Maurice Chevalier came out of retirement to record the film's title song.

Why not be a cool cat and claw at these questions for a while?

QUESTIONS

THE ARISTOCATS

1. Duchess is the lead cat character in this Disney classic. Who is Duchess's owner?

2. Duchess has three kittens. What are their names?

3. Duchess's owner wants to change her will to include the cats. Who is her lawyer?

4. In the event that the cats perish, who is to receive her money?

5. How does the movie's villain attempt to dispose of the cats?

6. What is the name of the house mouse in this film?

7. The villain's attempt to dump the cats in the country is foiled by two dogs. What are their names?

8. Who finds the lost cats and helps them on their journey?

9. Where, exactly, do the cats want to go?

10. Who encourages the house mouse to search for the missing cat family?

11. What are the names of the geese who save our alley-cat hero from drowning?

12. Why do these geese happen to be going to the very same place as our cat friends?

13. In what type of vehicle do the cats hide on their journey?

14. Upon arriving in the city, the cats are entertained by a cat jazz band singing what song?

15. Who is the leader of this band of cats?

16. Our villain makes yet another attempt to "lose" the cats when they finally arrive home. What is his plan?

17. Who saves the cats from this cruel fate, and how?

18. The cats' owner is so euphoric upon their safe return that she makes another generous gesture. What does she do?

19. What musical instrument does Duchess play in the film?

20. Who provides the voice of Duchess?

Answers on p. 203

ROBIN HOOD

Released: November 1973
Running Time: 83 Minutes

The release of *Robin Hood,* coincided with Walt Disney Productions's celebration of "50 Happy Years of Family Entertainment." Most unusual here was the matching of well-known characters to the particular types of animals that would portray them on the screen. The choices were perfect, and made for a very effective and different presentation of the Robin Hood legend. The songs, written by Roger Miller, Floyd Huddleston, George Burns, and Johnny Mercer, helped to re-create the England of that time. The ballad, "Love," received an Academy Award nomination for Best Song.

Will your aim be true as you set your sights on the questions that follow? We bet you're right on target!

QUESTIONS

ROBIN HOOD

1. Below is a list of five characters from *Robin Hood.* What types of animals represent these characters?
   a. Prince John
   b. Friar Tuck
   c. Little John
   d. Robin Hood
   e. The Sheriff of Nottingham

2. Who provided the voices for the following characters?
    a. The Rooster (story narrator)
    b. Little John
    c. Sir Hiss
    d. Prince John
    e. Friar Tuck

3. In the film, John does not often refer to his "outlaw" sidekick as Robin Hood, but uses a nickname instead. How does he refer to him?

4. How does Prince John obtain the royal crown?

5. How does Sir Hiss get Good King Richard to leave his kingdom?

6. What type of animal pulls the royal coach?

7. What type of animals are Prince John's "henchmen?"

8. The film shows Prince John on his way to Nottingham to collect taxes from the poor. On which road is the royal procession traveling?

9. What disguises do Robin Hood and Little John use in order to rob the royal procession of its ill-gotten bounty?

10. What does Prince John do any time anyone mentions his mother?

11. In the film, Little John sings a song entitled "The Phony King of England." What well-known composer wrote this tune?

12. How much is the reward offered for the capture of Robin Hood?

13. What is the name of Nottingham's village blacksmith, and what type of animal is he?

14. How old is Skippy the rabbit on the day the Sheriff of Nottingham steals Skippy's birthday present (one farthing) as payment for taxes due?

15. What gifts does Robin Hood give Skippy to make up for the callous deed of the Sheriff?

16. How does Robin Hood disguise himself in order to deliver these gifts?

17. One of Skippy's best friends is a turtle. What is his name?

18. Skippy and his turtle friend play at being what famous characters?

19. When Skippy attempts to retrieve his arrow from inside the castle walls, he comes upon Maid Marian and Lady Cluck, her lady-in-waiting, playing what sport?

20. What is unusual about the picture of Robin Hood that Maid Marian keeps in her chambers?

21. What prizes are offered to the winner of the championship archery tournament Prince John stages in order to capture Robin Hood?

22. As whom does Robin Hood enter the archery contest?

23. As whom does Little John pose in order to gain favor with Prince John at the tournament?

24. Who are the finalists at the tournament?

25. What type of animal plays the organ in Friar Tuck's church?

26. The sheriff of Nottingham arrests Friar Tuck for what fictitious crime?

27. What does Prince John do to attempt to capture Robin Hood after Friar Tuck's imprisonment?

28. What type of animal are Trigger and Nutsy, the palace guards, and who provided their voices, respectively, in the film?

29. What does palace guard Trigger call his beloved crossbow?

30. What joyous event takes place as the film closes?

Answers on p. 204

THE RESCUERS

Released: June 1977
Running Time: 76 Minutes

Walt Disney's talent-development program came to
fruition in a big way with the release of *The Rescuers*.
The program, initiated in 1970, enlisted talented young

animators to be trained by Disney veterans. By the time *The Rescuers* was released, some 30 animators had graduated from the program and were already making exciting contributions to the Disney tradition. *The Rescuers* was the first film to feature these new talents.

We hope you won't need to be rescued from the trivia questions that follow. Just do your very best on this Disney adventure.

QUESTIONS

THE RESCUERS

1. How does Penny get her message to the outside world that she is in trouble?

2. Who finds Penny's message; and where is it found?

3. After being read, where is the message taken?

4. A daring mouse named Bianca decides to rescue Penny. Whom does she choose as her partner in this adventure?

5. What is the name of the orphanage to which our sleuths are drawn?

6. Whom do they encounter upon arriving at the orphanage?

7. What evil woman is said to have been seen with Penny shortly before her disappearance?

8. What is the name of this evil woman's place of business?

9. Bianca overhears the evil woman disclose Penny's location. Where is she?

10. What form of transportation do Bianca and her partner use in order to reach Penny?

11. Upon reaching their destination, our sleuths are aided by two muskrats. What are their names?

12. Soon, all the "good guys" are being threatened by the evil woman's two pet crocodiles. Do you recall their names?

13. What is the name of the inept chap who assists the evil woman in this film?

14. How do the "bad guys" attempt to use Penny's small size to their advantage?

15. What is the name of the dragonfly who helps our sleuths in their quest to rescue little Penny?

16. What type of gem is our evil villain after, and what it is called?

17. Later, the gem is hidden in Penny's personal belongings. Where, exactly?

18. Aboard what vehicle do Penny and the others escape from Devil's Bayou?

19. What does Penny do when she returns home and realizes she has a valuable gem in her possession?

20. In what famous New York City building is the International Rescue Aid Society located?

Answers on p. 207

The **FOX** and the **Hound**

Released: July 1981
Running Time: 83 Minutes

The Fox and the Hound was the first film animated almost entirely by the new generation of Disney animators. At the time, it was the most expensive animated film ever produced—costing $12,000,000 and taking nearly four and a half years to complete. The story of these two friends who should be enemies is based on the popular book by Daniel P. Mannix.

Do you think you're sly enough to outsmart us by sniffing out answers to the following questions?

QUESTIONS

THE FOX AND THE HOUND

1. Who finds the little fox cub in the woods after its mother has been tracked and killed by a hunter?

2. Where does the character who finds the fox cub take him, and why?

3. What other characters help in transporting the fox cub?

4. What name does the fox cub's new human guardian give him?

5. What is the name of the hunter in this film?

6. The hunter has two dogs. Can you name them?

7. Which of these dogs befriends the fox cub and becomes best pals with him after only one day of frolicking in the woods?

8. Why is the fox cub's guardian forced to keep him indoors?

9. Where, eventually, does the guardian realize her young fox must go?

10. Soon, the young fox is reunited with the very same character who found him when the film began. Who provides the voice of this owl?

11. What is the name of the female fox the young fox falls in love with on sight? Who provides the voice for this character?

12. What does the young fox attempt in order to impress his fair lady?

13. In order to get rid of the fox, the hunter sets traps for him, only to fall into one of these traps himself. What causes this to happen?

14. Who saves the hunter from certain death in this scene?

15. Who provides the voice of the hunter in this film?

16. What song does the young fox's guardian sing to him when she takes him to the game preserve?

17. What is the name of the guardian's old cow?

18. In the film there is a caterpillar who, constantly being tormented by birds, finally outwits them by turning into a butterfly. What is this caterpillar-butterfly's name?

19. What favorite Disney actor provides the voice for the villain's younger dog as an adult?

20. Keith Mitchell provided the voice for the little fox cub. But a veteran actor was used to provide the voice for the older fox. Who was he?

Answers on p. 208

ᴛʜᴇ BLACK CAULDRON

Released: July 1985
Running Time: 80 Minutes

The Black Cauldron was somewhat unusual as far as Disney animated films are concerned. It told the story of good versus evil in a race to save humanity. The film cost approximately $25,000,000 to produce and was twelve years in the making—from drawing board to theater screen. It included some 2,519,200 drawings,

75,000 story sketches, and 2,000 miscellaneous sketches. It was the first animated film made in 70 mm since "Sleeping Beauty," 26 years before.

Now, we can't expect you to go out and save humanity like the heroes in this exciting film, but we do expect you to save face by answering at least a few of the following correctly.

QUESTIONS

THE BLACK CAULDRON

1. In what legendary kingdom does this film take place?

2. What evil power did the black cauldron possess?

3. Where does our young hero Taran live, and with whom?

4. What is Taran's occupation?

5. Whom does Taran long to fight?

6. Why is the evil king after Taran's pig?

7. On the journey to hide, and therefore protect his pig from the evil king, Taran drifts into a daydream. When he awakens, what odd little creature does he meet?

8. What types of animals are found chasing the oracular pig and finally capture her?

9. What creature threatens to execute the pig if she does not reveal the location of the black cauldron?

10. What happens to Taran as he tries to flee with the rescued pig?

11. What is the name of the beautiful princess Taran meets while imprisoned?

12. Where does Taran get the sword he carries as a weapon while attempting to escape from the castle?

13. What is the name of the minstrel rescued as he attempts to escape the castle?

14. Who is the king of the realm of the Fair Folk?

15. Where does the king say the black cauldron is hidden?

16. Who are the three witches of Morva?

17. What do the witches ask for in exchange for the cauldron?

18. Who sacrifices himself by throwing himself into the cauldron? (This is the only way to destroy its evil powers.)

19. How is the evil king killed?

20. After the evil powers are destroyed, the witches appear and want the cauldron back. What does Taran trade this time?

Answers on p. 210

THE GREAT MOUSE DETECTIVE

Released: July 1986
Running Time: 74 Minutes

The use of computer-assisted production techniques and an expanded staff of animators helped Disney Studios complete the animation for this film in just over a year—truly a remarkable feat. Common among the animators working on this film was their thorough enjoyment of the project. The storyline, based on the book by Eve Titus, easily lent itself to exaggerated character behavior and countless sight gags, and the animators reveled in it.

These questions are sure to separate the mice from the men, so go to it!

QUESTIONS

THE GREAT MOUSE DETECTIVE

1. What is special about the day on which the story begins?

2. What is Olivia Flaversham's father's name, and what is his occupation?

3. Who kidnaps Olivia's father, and why?

4. Who provides the voice of the evil Ratigan?

5. Who discovers Olivia upon his return to London?

6. Who is Olivia in the process of seeking out?

7. Where does this Great Mouse Detective live (hint: he has a rather famous neighbor)?

8. Who is The Great Mouse Detective's housekeeper?

9. What is the evil Ratigan's ultimate goal?

10. Who helps The Great Mouse Detective trace his quarry?

11. Where is Olivia when Ratigan's bat-henchman attempts to kidnap her?

12. The list the bat leaves behind is mistakenly traced to which London pub?

13. What does Dr. Dawson do after his drink at the pub is drugged?

14. When The Great Mouse Detective and Dr. Dawson are lured to Ratigan's lair, what becomes of them?

15. Why does the queen announce that she wants to marry Ratigan?

16. After his plot is exposed, how does Ratigan escape from the palace?

17. Ratigan's means of transport crashes into the face of a clock atop which building?

18. Who was The Great Mouse Detective's character named after?

19. What type of pet does Ratigan have in the film?

20. What type of animal is the juggler at The Rat Trap pub?

Answers on p. 211

DISNEY
ON
TELEVISION

Television made Walt Disney a household name. Through this medium, he was able to combine all forms of entertainment. "The Wonderful World of Disney" series, which aired under several titles, presented Disney with an open forum in which to entertain great numbers of viewers as he saw fit. Television also gave Walt Disney a chance to reach children in great numbers. He did this remarkably well with his classic creation, "The Mickey Mouse Club." Featuring youngsters as the principals on the program got young viewers involved in a special way.

Walt Disney never ran out of good ideas. Whether it was a Western-style serial, a nature film, scenes from animated classics, or a video trip through a theme park, it was exciting. Consequently, Disney television programming has kept millions glued to their sets for years.

Also in this next section, you'll find questions about four beloved Disney characters who made their public debuts in another medium, but achieved immortality through TV.

Initial Airing: October 1954

Beginning in 1954, Walt Disney brought a small slice of his genius into our living rooms every week via an anthology show, which began life as "Disneyland" (1954–58). The series continued for an unprecedented 29 seasons, making it the longest-running prime time program in TV history. Its other titles were "Walt Disney Presents" (1958–61), "Walt Disney's Wonderful World of Color" (1961–69), "The Wonderful World of Disney" (1969–79), "Disney's Wonderful World" (1979–81), and "Walt Disney" (1981–83).

WALT DISNEY PRESENTS

(1957–1961)

Can you match the following Disney productions with the actors who starred in them?

1. The Saga of Andy Burnett (1957)

2. Disneyland, The Park and Pecos Bill (1957)

3. The Nine Lives of Elfego Baca (1958)

4. Tales of Texas John Slaughter (1958)

5. The Boston Tea Party (1958)

6. The Peter Tchaikovsky Story (1959)

7. I Captured The King of the Leprechauns (1959)

8. The Birth of the Swamp Fox (1959)

9. Perilous Assignment (1959)

10. Rapids Ahead—Bear Country (1960)

11. Daniel Boone (1961)

a. Robert Loggia

b. Grant Williams

c. Leslie Nielsen

d. Michael Rennie

e. Roy Rogers

f. Dewey Martin

g. Hal Stalmaster

h. Tom Tryon

i. Jerome Courtland

j. Brian Keith

k. Pat O'Brien

Answers on p. 215

WALT DISNEY'S
WONDERFUL WORLD OF COLOR

(1961–1969)

Do you know who starred in the listed presentations featured on Walt "Disney's Wonderful World of Color"?

1. The Horsemasters (1961)

2. Backstage Party (1961)

3. Comanche (1962)

4. The Scarecrow of Romney Marsh (1964)

5. Treasure in the Haunted House (1964)

6. Kilroy (1965)

7. The Flight of the White Stallions (1965)

8. A Boy Called Nuthin' (1967)

9. Way Down Cellar (1968)

10. The Young Loner (1968)

11. Boomerang, Dog of Many Talents (1968)

12. The Treasure of San Bosco Reef (1968)

a. Ed Wynn

b. Sal Mineo

c. Butch Patrick

d. Celeste Holm

e. Darren McGavin

f. Ray Bolger

g. Patrick McGoohan

h. Kim Hunter

i. Annette Funicello

j. Forrest Tucker

k. James Daly

l. Robert Taylor

Answers on p. 215

THE WONDERFUL WORLD OF DISNEY

(1969–1979)

Match the feature to the actor who starred in it.

1. My Dog, the Thief (1969)
2. The Boy Who Stole the Elephant (1970)
3. The Wacky Zoo of Morgan City (1970)
4. Hacksaw (1971)
5. The Strange Monster of Strawberry Cove (1971)
6. The Mystery in Dracula's Castle (1973)
7. Rascal (1973)
8. Fire on Kelly Mountain (1973)
9. Run, Cougar, Run (1973)
10. Runaway on the Rogue River (1974)
11. The Boy Who Talked to Badgers (1975)
12. Kit Carson and the Mountain Men (1977)

a. Clu Gulager
b. Steve Forrest
c. Tab Hunter
d. Stuart Whitman
e. Dwayne Hickman
f. Christopher Connelly
g. Hal Holbrook
h. Burgess Meredith
i. Andrew Duggan
j. Slim Pickens
k. David Wayne
l. Carl Betz

Answers on p. 215

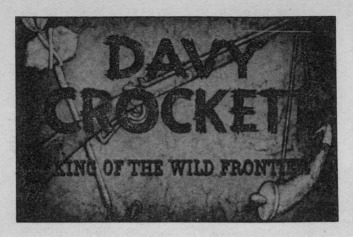

Initial Airing: December 1954

Although never becoming a series of its own, "Davy Crockett" was one of the most popular features on the Walt Disney program. It lifted its lead actor, Fess Parker, to virtual overnight stardom. Parker was totally believable as the honest, good-natured, completely pure "King of the Wild Frontier."

Everyone knows the song about Davy Crockett, but do you know how it came about? After shooting the series in Tennessee, Walt Disney realized he didn't have enough footage for three 60-minute shows. Walt suggested that the producer add some drawings and use them to introduce the show. Disney also realized that by itself the introduction was pretty dull. It needed a song to go with it. That song was "The Ballad of Davy Crockett," and, like the show, it became a hit.

Give the following questions your best shot.

QUESTIONS

DAVY CROCKETT

1. Who played Davy Crockett?

2. What is the name of the character played by Buddy Ebsen?

3. In the episode "Davy Crockett, Indian Fighter," who asks for Davy's help in defeating a band of Indians?

4. What is the name of the Indian chief who ambushes Major Tobias Norton and his troops?

5. Instead of killing this Indian chief, what does Davy Crockett do?

6. In what episode do we learn of Davy Crockett's wife?

7. In the second season, Davy runs a riverboat race. With whom does he compete?

8. What is Davy Crockett's motto?

9. In "Davy Crockett at the Alamo," who plays Colonel Jim Bowie?

10. What is the name of Davy Crockett's rifle?

Answers on p. 216

MICKEY MOUSE CLUB

Initial Airing: October 1955

At an original season cost of $15,000,000, Walt Disney brought this unique type of programming to TV and it was an instant success. Each hour-long program was broken up in this manner:

1. Introduction and newsreels
2. Mouseketeers and program guests
3. Live-action serials
4. Cartoon of the day

In the following section you will find trivia questions based on the ever-popular Mickey Mouse Club, so hold your banners high and go to it!

QUESTIONS

THE MICKEY MOUSE CLUB

1. Who is known as the Big Mooseketeer?

2. Who is the head Mouseketeer?

3. The selection of the young Mouseketeers was made by a group of four men. Who were they?

4. How much was a beginning Mouseketeer paid per week?

5. "The Mickey Mouse March" is heard at the beginning of every episode of "The Mickey Mouse Club." Who wrote this song?

6. Every day of the week is represented by a particular theme (activity) for each show. Try to match the activity with the particular day:

Monday	Circus Day
Tuesday	Talent Roundup Day
Wednesday	Fun with Music Day
Thursday	Guest Star Day
Friday	Anything Can Happen Day

7. At the start of "The Mickey Mouse Club's" first season, there were 24 Mouseketeers. When the show came to a close, only 9 members of the original 24 answered the roll call. How many of them can you name?

8. "The Mickey Mouse Club" introduced to us many entertaining serials. One was "The Hardy Boys." Who played them?

9. Probably the best-remembered serial is "The Adventures of Spin and Marty." Who played Spin? Marty?

10. What is Marty's real name?

11. What is the name of the boys' camp that served as the setting for this series?

12. Marty has a fear of horses but conquers it by riding what horse?

13. "Spin and Marty" was so popular, it inspired a sequel that added a neighboring girl's ranch to the plot. What two female Mouseketeers were featured in this sequel?

14. A new character, Moochie, was added to the "Spin and Marty" series. Who played Moochie?

15. Many members of "The Mickey Mouse Club" stayed in the entertainment industry. We will give a brief bio of what five particular members went on to do after "The Mickey Mouse Club." You tell us who they are.

a. played Chuck Connors's son on "The Rifleman"
b. was a regular on "My Three Sons" and starred in Disney's *The Shaggy Dog*
c. was a regular on "The Lawrence Welk Show"
d. was a regular orchestra member on "The Carol Burnett Show"
e. starred on "The Donna Reed Show"

Answers on p. 217

Initial Airing: October 1957

Walt Disney once again showed there were no limits to his abilities when he brought this exciting adventure series to television. The feel of it was so right—from the settings to the music—that it was a ratings smash from the outset. There were a total of 78 half-hour episodes of the "Zorro" series made, and the cost of production bordered on $6,000,000. "Zorro" is still being seen on The Disney Channel.

There are usually interesting stories associated with programs that prominently feature animals, and "Zorro" is no exception. Zorro's chief horse was actually four horses—that is, there were four identical horses on the set, each possessing the ability to perform different skills called for in the scripts. All four were used as their particular strengths were needed. Combined, they added up to the perfect four-legged companion for our debonair hero.

So saddle up, jump on your trusty stallion (whichever one you think would be the best at trivia), and go hard at the following questions.

QUESTIONS

ZORRO (1957–1959 ON ABC)

1. Who plays the title role of Zorro in this exciting adventure series?

2. Although "Zorro" has become a household word and many people use it to refer to our hero, it of course is not his real name. What is Zorro's real name?

3. In what year is this series set?

4. What Western state functions as the setting?

5. Zorro returns home because his father requests him to. Where has he been living?

6. What is Zorro's father's name, and what actor portrays him?

7. What is the name of the wicked commandant who has taken control of the Fortress de los Angeles? (He soon becomes Zorro's arch enemy, upon Zorro's return home.)

8. This wicked commandant has a rotund sidekick. Can you name that sidekick and the actor who portrays him in the series?

9. Zorro also has a sidekick. A mute, he pretends to be deaf as well in order to gain information for his master. Can you name this character and the actor who plays him?

10. What is Zorro's trademark?

11. In the second season of the series, a love interest was introduced for our hero. Can you recall her name?

12. Zorro has two horses. Can you name them? (One is black, the other white.)

13. Annette Funicello, a favorite of Walt Disney lovers the world over, also has a role in the series. Can you name the character Annette portrays?

14. What is the name of the theme song used for the "Zorro" series?

15. This song was a top hit in 1958. What is the name of the group that made the hit recording of the song?

Answers on p. 218

A Special Tribute
To
Mickey Mouse
Donald Duck
Goofy
Pluto

Both the early Walt Disney series and "The Mickey Mouse Club" featured cartoon segments with Disney's all-time favorite animated characters. We felt it would be criminal not to pay a special tribute to these superstars created by Walt Disney Studios. Although they may be a little on in years, they will always remain young in our hearts, and, more important, they keep us young at heart.

On the following pages, you will find trivia questions about these four beloved characters. We hope you enjoy the memories these questions conjure up as you try to summon the correct answers.

QUESTIONS

MICKEY MOUSE

1. Mickey's first film was also the first animated film to have a fully synchronized soundtrack. Do you know the name of the film?

2. In which film does Mickey crash a plane, but not before he's sure Minnie Mouse is safely parachuting her way to earth?

3. In *Magician Mickey* (1937), Mickey runs into a little trouble after attempting a trick with Donald Duck as the subject. What kind of a mess does Mickey create in this film?

4. In *Mr. Mouse Takes a Trip* (1940), whom does Mickey take along with him by stuffing him into his luggage?

5. What film, based on a Grimm fairy tale, shows Mickey performing one heroic deed after another?

6. What was the first Mickey Mouse film to be shot in Technicolor?

7. One Mickey Mouse film, which featured a grammatical error in its title, was made in black-and-white in 1934 and again in color in 1941. Do you know the title of this film?

8. On what classic story is *Thru the Mirror* (1936) based?

9. What role does Mickey Mouse play in the 1940 Disney film classic *Fantasia*?

10. What is the name of Mickey's record album that, released in 1979, went "multi-platinum"?

11. In what film does Mickey utter his first words?

12. *Lend a Paw* (1941) features Mickey and his pal Pluto. This film is a remake of a short made in 1933. Can you recall the title of the original?

13. In what film is Mickey represented as a football hero?

14. In *Mickey's Orphans* (1931), what does Mickey find on his doorstep Christmas Eve?

15. What chore gives Mickey trouble in *Mickey's Service Station* (1935)?

16. Over what character does Mickey triumph in *Mickey's Rival* (1936)?

17. In what film do Mickey and Pluto first appear together?

18. Who decides to "make a home" in Mickey and Pluto's Christmas tree in *Pluto's Christmas Tree* (1952)?

19. After a thirty-year absence, Mickey returned to the big screen in what 1983 Disney production?

20. What role does Mickey play in his 1983 comeback?

Answers on p. 219

QUESTIONS

DONALD DUCK

1. What is the name of Donald's first film?

2. What two poems does Donald recite in *Orphan's Benefit* (1934)?

3. Donald is given a love interest in *Don Donald* (1937). Who is she?

4. In what film does Donald appear as a solo star for the first time?

5. What is the underlying message to the audience in *Donald's Decision* (1942)?

6. Which of Donald's films prompts folks to file their income tax and pay their fair share?

7. One of Donald's films won an Academy Award for Best Cartoon Short Subject. Do you know which one?

8. Do you remember what subject is parodied in *Donald's Dilemma* (1947)?

9. In *Chef Donald* (1941), what error does Donald make while attempting to prepare waffles?

10. What does Donald steal in the film *Donald's Crime* (1945)?

11. In the film *Duck Pimples* (1945), what is Donald seen hallucinating about?

12. In which of Donald's films is his lunch devoured by a troop of hungry ants?

13. What are the names of Donald's three nephews?

14. What is the name of the film in which these three little duckie darlings make their film debut?

15. *Saludos Amigos* is a Disney production made up of several featurettes saluting South America. In a sequence called "Lake Titicaca," what country does Donald tour?

16. In another sequence in the same film, Donald meets up with a character named José Carioca. What type of animal is José?

17. Donald appears briefly as a farmer in a sequence in *The Reluctant Dragon* (1941). What is his character's name?

18. Donald is reunited with José Carioca in a feature called *Melody Time* (1948). What sequence contains these two characters?

19. In the film *The Three Caballeros* (1945), who are the three *caballeros*?

20. Donald falls for not one ... not two ... but three women in *The Three Caballeros*. Can you name them?

Answers on p. 221

GOOFY

1. In what film does Goofy make his screen debut?

2. What is the name of the 1932 film in which Goofy assists Mickey Mouse in preparing food for a party?

3. In the 1935 film *Mickey's Service Station,* what function does Goofy serve at the station?

4. How does Goofy attempt to catch fish in *On Ice* (1935)?

5. In *Moving Day* (1936), what item does Goofy have a great deal of trouble loading onto the mover's truck?

6. In *Moose Hunters* (1937), Donald Duck and Goofy wear a moose costume. Which half is Goofy?

7. What perfume do the boys use to attract a moose in *Moose Hunters*?

8. Goofy's first solo starring performance is in *Goofy and Wilbur* (1939). Who is Wilbur?

9. In *Foul Hunting* (1947), what is the name of Goofy's live duck decoy?

10. From what Disney feature is the film short "How to Ride a Horse?"

11. What is Goofy's horse's name in this film?

12. Goofy appears in several public-service shorts dealing with safe driving. What names are given to Goofy in these films to mock some of our poor driving habits?

13. What is the name of the 1946 film that has Goofy showing us all about basketball?

14. What female character does Goofy dress as in *A Knight for a Day* (1946)?

15. What is Goofy's son's name?

16. What is Goofy's wife's name?

17. What role does Goofy play in *Mickey's Christmas Carol* (1983)?

18. What was Goofy's original name in the comic strips?

19. What film has Goofy precariously walking on the ledge of a rather tall structure?

20. What is the title of Goofy's film on hockey?

Answers on p. 222

PLUTO

1. In what film does Pluto make his first appearance for Disney, although he remains unnamed in the plot?

2. In Pluto's second film, *The Picnic* (1930), he goes by another name. What is that name?

3. Although in later years it is clearly established that Pluto is Mickey Mouse's dog, whose dog is he in *The Picnic*?

4. In *Lend a Paw* (1941), Pluto pulls a bag from the river. What, to his disgust, is in the bag?

5. In the same film, Pluto makes a mess by causing Mickey's fishbowl to topple. What is the name of Mickey's goldfish?

6. In *Pluto's Judgment Day* (1935), Pluto dreams that he is on trial. What is unusual about the jury his mind conjures up?

7. In *Mickey's Grand Opera* (1936), Pluto ruins an operatic performance by what two characters?

8. Pluto attempts to steal a large bone from an animal cage in *Pluto at the Zoo* (1942). What type of animal inhabits the cage?

9. What Pluto film on TV features Pappy Coyote, Junior Coyote, and Grandpappy Coyote?

10. What is the name of Pluto's heartthrob in *Pluto's Heartthrob* (1950)?

11. What is the first movie Pluto appears in where he is known, in fact, as Pluto?

12. In 1941, Pluto appeared in a film with Mickey Mouse. The subject was golf. Do you recall the name of the film?

13. In the film *On Ice* (1935), one Disney character humiliates Pluto by putting ice skates on him while he sleeps, waking him up suddenly, and watching him flounder all over the ice. What character deals Pluto this cruel fate?

14. Who is Pluto's first great love?

15. What is the name of the kitten that drives Pluto absolutely nuts on occasion in several Disney short subjects?

Answers on p. 224

DISNEY'S
FEATURE
FILMS

With their wonderful theater releases, the Disney Studios have long set the tone for family entertainment. Always a guiding force, Walt Disney's personal dedication to family entertainment is still very much a priority on current production schedules. And in an age when exploitative, violence-packed cinema makes a strong statement, each new Disney release makes us that much more grateful.

For four decades we have laughed and cried as we've watched familiar faces on the big screen perform great antics. Actors who appeared in a Walt Disney film tended to return to star in other Disney ventures as well. In a very real sense they became part of a larger Disney family, and, in an extended sense, part of ours. They cemented our own sense of family solidarity.

We were always thrilled to see Fred MacMurray, Dean Jones, or Keenan Wynn entertaining us. We just knew we would be in for a treat when their names, among others, lighted the marquee.

Some of the most enjoyable moments we can recall are rooted in the following features.

Treasure Island

Released: July 1950
Running Time: 96 Minutes

Anyone even remotely familiar with the story of *Treasure Island* remembers Long John Silver's parrot. It was his constant companion. During the shooting of this film, the parrot decided to take leave of the cast and set up housekeeping in a nearby tree. No amount of effort could coax the bird back to the set, so a replacement was called for. Only when he saw that his role was about to be handed to another bird did the parrot return, allowing filming to begin again.

Go ahead and dig up the precious memories buried deep in your mind and answer these questions based on Disney's classic live-action adaption of a beloved pirate tale.

QUESTIONS

TREASURE ISLAND

1. This classic is based on a book written by what famous author?

2. In what country, and in what year, does this movie open?

3. As the film opens, we see a man entering an inn. What is the name of the inn?

4. Who is this man who is looking for Captain Billy Bones?

5. What is the name of the boy whose mother runs the inn?

6. How does the man know the boy is lying when he says Captain Bones isn't there?

7. What alcohol is consumed by two of the three characters we have seen up to this point in the film?

8. In the next sequence of the film, what "gift" is the captain given from all his shipmates?

9. When Captain Bones collapses and sends the boy for help, what item does he also entrust to him?

10. Whom does the boy return with to assist the captain, who is pronounced dead?

11. What is the name of the ship on which our cast sets out to find the treasure?

12. Who is hired as the sea cook for the voyage?

13. What is the name of the captain chosen to command the voyage?

14. What is the name of the ship's first mate? In the film, who kills this character?

15. What is the penalty for carrying a concealed weapon aboard the ship?

16. How does the ship's captain learn of the plans for mutiny?

17. Even though the mutiny fails, the pirates do come out of it with a hostage for bargaining power. Who is this hostage?

18. What is the name of the man who has been marooned on the island, and how long has he been there?

19. When the second attempt at mutiny is a success, what symbolic gesture do the pirates make of its completion?

20. What fruit does the pirate leader tell us should be consumed to fight off scurvy?

21. When the pirates are ready to travel to the island, which two are told to stay behind and watch the ship?

22. The boy sneaks back to the ship at nightfall to cut the anchor line. This will cause the ship to drift and ground itself. He is knifed before he leaves the ship, but manages to do what before he returns to the island?

23. What does the pirate crew give their leader as they grow anxious over the treasure they so desperately want to find?

24. Why is the treasure missing when the pirates eventually dig for it?

25. What gift does the pirate leader attempt to give the boy as he is being taken into custody?

Answers on p. 229

20,000 Leagues
UNDER THE Sea

Released: December 1954
Running Time: 127 Minutes

Many aspects of the underwater film techniques used to film *20,000 Leagues Under the Sea* are simply mind-boggling. It was quite an undertaking by Disney, but, as usual, the results made for perfect entertainment. At one point there were 42 cast and crew members on the ocean floor. This movie was filmed partially on location in Nassau and Montego Bay, Jamaica.

Don't get swept away in the trivia currents as you dive into the following questions.

QUESTIONS

20,000 LEAGUES UNDER THE SEA

1. *20,000 Leagues Under the Sea* is based on a celebrated novel penned by what famous science fiction writer?

2. In what year does this film take place?

3. What is the name of the first ship destroyed by the so-called Sea Monster?

4. Who is the captain of the submarine *Nautilus*? What award-winning actor plays him?

5. What role does Kirk Douglas play in this film, and what is his character's occupation?

6. What is the name of the professor who is searching for the Sea Monster?

7. Who played the professor's trustworthy apprentice, Conseil?

8. Throughout the film, we hear Kirk Douglas singing and whistling a tune. What is its title?

9. The professor is a member of what museum, and where is his search going to take him?

10. How many Academy awards did this film win, and what were they?

11. The food on the *Nautilus* actually comes from the ocean floor. Can you tell us what makes up the following?
    a. cream
    b. pudding

12. What main dish does Captain Nemo serve to the professor and his friends on their first night aboard the *Nautilus*?

13. Where is the crew when the professor and his friends first come aboard the *Nautilus*?

14. On board the *Nautilus,* what is the name of the seal who befriends Kirk Douglas?

15. Of what are Captain Nemo's cigars made?

16. Where does the crew of the *Nautilus* do its farming?

17. According to the story, where was the *Nautilus* built, and who built her?

18. According to Captain Nemo, when the ship is under attack by a gigantic squid, he tells his crew to work on the squid's only vital spot. What is it?

19. Who eventually saves Captain Nemo from the squid?

20. Where and how does Captain Nemo die?

Answers on p. 231

OLD YELLER

Released: December 1957
Running Time: 83 Minutes

This film featured an absolutely incredible acting job by its title character, Old Yeller himself. Yeller was played by a dog named Spike, a 115-pound canine from the kennels of Frank and Rudd Weatherwax, owners and trainers of Lassie, among other star dogs. Frank Weatherwax found Spike in a Van Nuys, California pound in 1953 and bailed him out for three dollars. Four years later, Spike was a major

Hollywood celebrity and the true star of one of the most poignant movies ever made.

Time to "bone" up on *Old Yeller.* Go "fetch!"

QUESTIONS

OLD YELLER

1. In what state does this film take place?

2. Who plays the role of Jim Coates, and why is he absent during most of this film?

3. Who plays the role of Katie Coates?

4. When first we see Old Yeller, what is he doing?

5. What are the Coateses' two children's names?

6. Years before Yeller, the Coates family had another dog. What was the dog's name?

7. What is the name of the mule in the film?

8. At first, Travis hates Yeller. What trap does he set in order to have reason to shoot him?

9. How does Yeller save the youngest Coates boy?

10. Who is left behind by the men of the town to "protect" the women and children while they are on their cattle drive?

11. What secret about Yeller does Lisbeth Searcy know?

12. Lisbeth promises not to tell, but to be sure, Travis gives her something. What does he give her?

13. Why do Travis and Yeller sleep in the corn patch?

14. In the film, one of the Coateses' cows gives birth. What is the cow's name?

15. Burn Sanderson comes to the Coateses' home looking for his dog (Yeller). Who plays the role of Burn Sanderson?

16. Seeing how attached the family is to Yeller, Burn "trades" him for what items?

17. What disease does Burn tell Travis is sweeping the countryside?

18. What type of animal attacks both Travis and Yeller?

19. What does Katie use to stitch Old Yeller's wounds?

20. Why is Travis forced to shoot Yeller?

21. What gift does Jim bring his wife when he returns home from the cattle drive?

22. What gifts does he bring his children?

Answers on p. 232

Pollyanna

Released: May 1960
Running Time: 134 Minutes

Over the years Disney Studios got a reputation for featuring the same family of actors in its films. The audiences' familiarity with these stars added to the enjoyment of watching a Disney film. Unusually, eight of "Pollyanna's" nine stars were making their first appearance in a Disney film. Authenticity and attention to detail were key, as set designers took great care in recreating homes from the 1912 era. They even used a real train from that time, supplied by the Western Pacific Railroad.

The child star of this Disney film received an honorary Academy Award for her outstanding performance. Will your performance be as outstanding as you attempt to answer the following questions?

QUESTIONS

POLLYANNA

1. Who wrote *Pollyanna*?

2. Who is Nancy's boyfriend in the film?

3. What is Mr. Thomas's position at Polly's house in Harrington?

4. What did Pollyanna's father do for a living?

5. At what hour does Aunt Polly have dinner?

6. What is Pollyanna's favorite game?

7. Why does Pollyanna come to live with her aunt?

8. Who is the upstairs maid?

9. Why does Aunt Polly buy new clothes for Pollyanna?

10. What is Pollyanna's last name?

11. Name the doctor who comes back to Harrington after many years away.

12. Who is the reverend of the local church in Harrington?

13. What is the mayor's first name?

14. According to the reverend's sermon, what comes unexpectedly?

15. Name the orphan who is Pollyanna's friend.

16. Name the actress who played Mrs. Snow.

17. What is Mrs. Snow's daughter's name?

18. For what are the profits from the bazaar to be used?

19. What does Mrs. Snow make for the bazaar?

20. According to Pollyanna, how many times has God told us to be glad?

21. Reverend Ford finds even more happy texts. How many does he find?

22. What is Pollyanna's favorite dessert?

23. What type of accident does Pollyanna have?

24. What does Pollyanna get at the bazaar's fishing pond?

25. Where does Pollyanna have to go for an operation?

26. Who adopts Jimmy Bean?

27. According to the residents of Harrington, what does Pollyanna give the people?

28. According to the sign at the train station, what is the new nickname for Harrington?

29. Where in town do the water pipes burst?

30. What fascinates and delights Pollyanna in Mr. Pendergast's home?

Answers on p. 234

The Absent-minded Profesor

Released: March 1961
Running Time: 97 Minutes

Long-time vaudeville star Belle Montrose made her film debut as the absent minded professor's housekeeper in this favorite Disney feature. But perhaps her most outstanding contribution to the field of entertainment was bringing her son, Steve Allen, into the world.

Now, don't be absent-minded while attempting to answer the following trivia questions.

QUESTIONS

THE ABSENT MINDED PROFESSOR

1. What actor played the title role in this Disney favorite?

2. What is the absent minded professor's real name in the film?

3. Where does the absent minded professor teach?

4. What subject does the absent minded professor teach?

5. As the film opens, what principle is the absent minded professor seen explaining?

6. Who is the absent minded professor supposed to marry?

7. Who wants to steal her away from the absent minded professor?

8. Why is everyone unsure that this wedding will take place?

9. What is the name of the professor's housekeeper?

10. The professor has a dog. What's his name?

11. Why does the professor miss his wedding this time?

12. What does the professor discover in his garage-laboratory?

13. What is the name of the developer who wants to tear down the college and build a housing tract?

14. Who is president of the college where the professor teaches?

15. To what unusual use does the professor put his new discovery?

16. The professor also uses his discovery to give his school's basketball team a "lift." Trailing 46–3 at half time, the team eventually wins the game. What is the final score?

17. Who spots the professor using his "secret" discovery?

18. How do they attempt to steal the professor's secret?

19. What nickname do the students have for the absent minded professor?

20. When the professor calls the President of the United States to tell of his discovery, who, instead does he talk to on the phone?

21. What musical instrument does the professor walk into while attempting to steal back his stolen discovery?

22. Who plays the role of the local fire chief?

Answers on p. 235

The
PARENT TRAP!

Released: June 1961
Running Time: 124 Minutes

The Parent Trap is considered by many to be Walt Disney's funniest family film. From subtle sarcasm to out-and-out slapstick, this fast-paced movie generates nonstop laughs. As a Disney ad for it states:

"Dedicated to the proposition that teen-agers and adults are created equally hilarious!"

You can ask Mommy and Daddy for help if need be, as you try to avoid the trivia traps while answering the following questions.

QUESTIONS

THE PARENT TRAP

1. Who plays the dual role of Sharon McKendrick/Susan Evers in this Disney film?

2. Who plays the roles of Mitch Evers and Margaret (Maggie) McKendrick, the girls' parents?

3. At what summer camp do the girls meet and realize they are twins who were separated as infants due to divorce?

4. What "Beverly Hillbillies" star plays the counselor at the camp registration desk?

5. Who are Sharon's roommates at summer camp?

6. What is the name of the bunkhouse they share?

7. It is announced that a nearby boys' camp will be participating in a dance on the coming weekend. What is the name of this boys' camp?

8. In what states do Sharon and Susan live, respectively?

9. What is the girls' punishment for brawling at the dance?

10. How are they convinced they are truly sisters?

11. What is the twins' birthday?

12. What is the name of Susan's dog, and what type of dog is he?

13. Mitch Evers has both a loyal housekeeper and ranch hand. Can you name the characters who filled these positions?

14. What do the girls decide to do in order to get to know the mother or father they never had?

15. What nasty habit does Sharon have to take up in order to make their plan work?

16. What gifts does Susan bring home to her grandmother in Boston?

17. The girls plot to get information on how their parents met in an attempt to reunite them. Where, do they find out, Mitch took Maggie on their first date?

18. Sharon goes to California, only to find her father planning to marry Vicky Robinson. Who plays the role of Miss Robinson?

19. Why is Mitch's family against his new marriage plans?

20. What nickname does Mitch Evers have for his daughter Susan?

21. How does the girls' grandfather learn of their plan?

22. Before returning to California, why do Susan and her mother stop off in New York?

23. What is the name of the reverend who will supposedly be marrying Mitch and Vicky?

24. Sharon and Susan try to recreate their parents' first date. What does the housekeeper make for dinner to help with their plan?

25. What song do the girls perform during dinner?

26. How do the girls delay their mother's departure for Boston?

27. The girls are determined to scare Vicky away. On a camping trip, what animal do they plant on a canteen in order to frighten her?

28. When the girls cover Vicky's feet with honey, what animals delight in licking it up?

29. What do the girls, their father, and Vicki have for dinner on their first night of camping?

30. What does the final scene find the girls doing?

Answers on p. 237

Babes in Toyland

Released: December 1961
Running Time: 105 Minutes

Babes in Toyland was Walt Disney's first live-action, full-length musical. The fantasy usually associated with Disney animation was brought to the big screen in this film via actors in miniature and toys coming to life. It set the stage for the live-action fantasy films that followed.

Get ready for the adventure of a lifetime as you take a journey to Toyland through trivia.

QUESTIONS

BABES IN TOYLAND

1. Who wrote the operetta *Babes in Toyland*?

2. Who directed the Disney classic *Babes in Toyland*?

3. Who is Sylvester?

4. Where does Tom and Mary's wedding take place?

5. What actress plays Little Bo Peep?

6. What actors play the roles of Tom and Mary?

7. What drink is served in the beginning of the film as the town prepares for Tom and Mary's wedding?

8. Name the character played by Ray Bolger.

9. Who played the toy maker?

10. Whom does Barnaby plan on kidnapping?

11. What does Barnaby plan to do with Tom's body?

12. What color ribbon does Mary wear in the garden one starry night when she sings "Just a Whisper Away"?

13. What is the shape of the glass on Mary's front door?

14. What is Mary's last name?

15. Little Bo Peep's sheep got lost in the forest. Can you name it?

16. Why is Toyland closed?

17. What is so unique about the trees in the Forest of No Return?

18. Who plays the toy maker's assistant?

19. What time is it when the toy machine explodes?

20. What is the first item to be shrunk by the toymaker?

21. Who is the mayor of Toyland?

22. What does Tom ride as he and the wooden soldiers attack Barnaby?

23. Who shoots Barnaby with a boat cannon?

24. What color cape does Mary wear on her wedding day?

25. Describe, in one word, the weather on Tom and Mary's wedding day.

Answers on p. 239

MARY POPPINS

Released: August 1964
Running Time: 140 Minutes

With the release of *Mary Poppins*, Walt Disney took a glorious piece of the past and brought it into the present, reviving the feature film musical that was so popular in the '30s and '40s. Special to *Mary Poppins* were animated sequences featuring live actors (sort of a reverse of the method used in *Song of the South*, where animated characters appeared in a live sequence).

QUESTIONS

MARY POPPINS

1. Who wrote *Mary Poppins*?

2. Name the street where the Bankses live.

3. What is the number on the front door of the Bankses' home?

4. What positions are held by Mrs. Brill and Ellen in the Banks home?

5. Whose house is built just like a ship?

6. How many children does George Banks have, and what are their names?

7. At what time of morning does Admiral Boom fire his cannon?

8. Mary Poppins carries what two items when she arrives at the home of George Banks?

9. Who do Mary and the children meet in the park?

10. According to Mary Poppins, what helps the medicine go down?

11. Who serves refreshments to Mary and Bert on their Jolly Holiday?

12. From what does Uncle Albert suffer?

13. Where do Uncle Albert, Mary, Bert, and the children have a tea party one day?

14. Name the song that is also the name of the place George Banks takes the children for a day's outing?

15. Where does the old bird woman sell her bags of crumbs for tuppence?

16. Who is the chairman of the British bank where George Banks works?

17. Name the two characters Dick Van Dyke plays.

18. Name the Oscar-winning song sung by Mary and Bert on the rooftops of London.

19. What type of pictures does Bert draw on the sidewalks?

20. According to Mary Poppins, what is the only word to use when nothing else will do?

21. As soon as *it* changes, Mary Poppins tells the children, she will leave. To what is she referring?

22. Who is the only person to see Mary Poppins fly away?

23. What is so unique about Mary Poppins's umbrella besides the fact that one is able to fly with it?

24. What is Mary Poppins's favorite flavor of ice?

25. What is George Banks's wife's name?

Answers on p. 241

THE Gnome-MOBILE

Released: July 1967
Running Time: 90 Minutes

The Gnome-Mobile marked the last appearance in a Disney film for long-time favorite Ed Wynn. This film was Wynn's eighth for Disney Studios, and it was completed just five months before his death. Wynn's role in *The Gnome-Mobile* was that of a jovial two-foot-tall gnome. Some of Wynn's other film appearance included roles in *The Absent Minded Professor, Babes in Toyland,* and *Mary Poppins.*

Spin your small wheels on the following questions.

QUESTIONS

THE GNOME-MOBILE

1. What two roles did Walter Brennan play in this film?

2. What award-winning Disney team wrote the *Gnome-Mobile* theme song?

3. Where do the gnomes live?

4. The film deals with one particular gnome named Jasper, who has a big problem for a tiny person. What is his problem?

5. To whom does Jasper first speak about his problem? (Hint: It is not a gnome.)

6. What is the expression gnomes use for humans?

7. What kind of car is the gnome-mobile?

8. Who kidnaps the gnomes so he can use them in his show?

9. Where are they kidnapped from, and to what show are we referring?

10. Who does Knobby feel is ruining the forest?

11. Who is the head of D. J. Mulrooney's security staff, and what character actor plays him?

12. Where is Horatio Quaxton's mountain cabin located?

13. At one point in the film, we see the gnome-mobile is taken to the local service station. What does it need?

14. Where is D.J. taken when he tells people about the gnomes?

15. Who helps D.J. escape?

16. What is the name of the guard dog at the sanitarium?

17. When Jasper is brought to a new forest of gnomes, we are introduced to Rufus, who finally helps Jasper with his problem. What favorite Disney actor played the role of Rufus?

18. According to Rufus, describe the "gnome law" as it governs the matching up of boy and girl gnome.

19. Whom does Jasper finally take for his wife?

20. What does D. J. Mulrooney give the gnomes as a wedding present?

Answers on p. 242

The Happiest Millionaire

Released: June 1967 (premiere)
Running Time: 164 Minutes

The Biddle mansion featured in this film cost close to $500,000 to build, and was one of the most expensive interior sets ever created by Walt Disney Productions. Among the many antiques contained in the house was a desk said to have been used by Napoleon. It would be conservative to estimate that the same endeavor today would cost ten times as much.

We spared no expense in compiling the following questions, so we don't expect you to be stingy with the correct answers.

QUESTIONS

THE HAPPIEST MILLIONAIRE

1. What Academy Award-winning team wrote the music and lyrics for *The Happiest Millionaire*?

2. *The Happiest Millionaire* will be remembered for its great period costumes. Who designed the costumes?

3. In what year does the film open?

4. In what city do the Biddles live?

5. Name the song sung by Tommy Steele in the film's opening.

6. Where does Mrs. Duke live?

7. Who plays John Lawless?

8. Name the employment agency that recommends Mr. Lawless to the Biddles.

9. For what position does Mr. Lawless interview at the Biddleses?

10. Who played Mrs. Worth? (Hint: she was also in "Mary Poppins")

11. Name the Oscar-winning actress who played Mrs. Duke.

12. On what type of diet is Anthony J. Drexel Biddle when we first see him?

13. What is printed on the sweatshirts worn by Mr. Biddle and his daughter?

14. What is Mr. Biddle's daughter's name?

15. How many sons do Mr. and Mrs. Biddle have, and what are their names?

16. What is the name of Mr. Biddle's favorite alligator?

17. What do Cordy's brothers do to her date?

18. According to Mr. Biddle, which one of his children has the best left hook?

19. How many pet alligators does Mr. Biddle have, and where did he get them?

20. What is the name of the school for girls that Cordy attends, and where is it located?

21. Who is Cordy's roommate?

22. From what country does John Lawless come?

23. Name the two boys who are introduced to Cordy by Aunt Mary.

24. What kind of dance does Cordy think is for old people?

25. Name the U.S. President who makes headlines in the newspaper *The Evening Bulletin.*

26. Name the two female characters who sing "There Are Those."

27. Who played Aunt Mary?

28. What does John Lawless offer Aunt Mary and Mrs. Duke while they serve each other verbal poison darts?

29. Name the bar that John Lawless and Angier Duke attend.

30. What do John and Angier drink at the bar?

Answers on p. 244

THE LOVE BUG

Released: March 1969
Running Time: 107 Minutes

Only Disney could have a smash hit with a movie based on the exploits of a 1963 Volkswagen Beetle named Herbie. Actually, this film was delightfully done and has inspired several sequels. In fact, Herbie's tire prints were captured in cement in front of Hollywood's famous Chinese Theatre.

Herbie had a souped-up motor enabling him to reach speeds of up to 150 mph. Try to come up with some speedy answers to the following questions.

QUESTIONS

THE LOVE BUG

1. Who plays the role of race-car driver Jim Douglas in this film?

2. Who plays the role of his romantic interest, Carole Bennett?

3. What is the name of the eccentric mechanic played by comedian Buddy Hackett?

4. As the film opens, Jim Douglas is seen crashing a car. What is the number of this car?

5. What, does Jim complain, is the only food his roommate keeps in the house?

6. Where did Buddy Hackett's character go to find his "real self"?

7. What car is Jim Douglas fascinated with when he visits the car dealership?

8. What is the license plate number on Herbie, the Love Bug?

9. How does Herbie get his name?

10. Where does Herbie drive Jim and Carole the first time they are in the car together?

11. What is the name of the local "make-out" spot in the film?

12. When Jim decides to race Herbie, what number is the car given?

13. How does Herbie show his dislike for Mr. Thorndyke, the dealer who sold him?

14. At which racetrack does Herbie achieve a new record-qualifying time?

15. At which other track does Herbie set an actual track record?

16. When asked which part of Ireland his mother came from, how does Buddy Hackett respond?

17. How does Mr. Thorndyke attempt to sabotage Herbie?

18. What type of car does Jim Douglas buy after he is convinced Herbie's had it?

19. How does Herbie attempt to "commit suicide"?

20. Who becomes Herbie's new owner after he destroys the shop?

21. Who is Thorndyke's driving partner in the big race that is the film's finale?

22. What city serves as the midpoint and overnight rest stop during the big race?

23. What is the number of the car Thorndyke is driving?

Answers on p. 245

Bedknobs and Broomsticks

Released: November 1971
Running Time: 139 Minutes

Bedknobs and Broomsticks was another Disney film that combined live-action with animation. In fact, one 22-minute animated sequence took nearly one year and close to $2,000,000 to complete. *Bedknobs and Broomsticks* was the seventh Walt Disney film on which producer Bill Walsh and director Robert Stevenson had collaborated.

Grab your broomsticks and get ready to fly off on another trivia adventure.

QUESTIONS

BEDKNOBS AND BROOMSTICKS

1. In what country and in what year is this Disney film set?

2. Who played the role of Miss Eglantine Price in this film?

3. As the film opens, a British army officer is seen asking directions to what city?

4. The local museum has been closed and is now being used as what type of facility?

5. Miss Price is informed that she must provide a home for three children. What are their names?

6. Miss Price picks up a package at the local postal station. From whom does the package come?

7. What does the package contain?

8. What type of unusual vehicle does Miss Price drive? What is her license plate number? (Sorry, we got carried away!)

9. What is the name of Miss Price's black cat?

10. What spell is needed to make Miss Price's flying broomstick fly?

11. In order to prove herself a witch to be reckoned with, into what does Miss Price turn one of the children?

12. Miss Price wants the children to keep her secret about being a witch so she entrusts them with a spell. Which spell is it?

13. Why does Miss Price travel to London to find Professor Browne?

14. Professor Browne does not believe the bed can fly until Miss Price and the children give him a ride home. Where does Professor Browne live?

15. What is the name of the book that contains the all-important last spell that Miss Price is determined to learn?

16. What is Miss Price unhappy to learn when she locates the book?

17. What type of spell is it with which Miss Price is so obsessed?

18. Professor Browne takes Miss Price to a street flea market to find the missing book. On what street is this flea market?

19. The book with the spell is not found, but a legend is. The spell is on the Star of Astaroth (a medallion), which legend says was taken from Astaroth by a group of wild animals that killed him and set off to their own island. What is the name of this island run by wild animals?

20. When Miss Price, Professor Browne, and the children travel to this animal-run island, what type of animal do they find to be king?

21. How does Professor Browne get on the king's good side?

22. Where do our travelers find the Star of Astaroth?

23. What is the name of the team for which the king plays soccer?

24. What type of animal acts as a medic at the soccer game?

25. What is the spell that puts Substitutiary Locomotion into effect?

26. When Nazi soldiers stage a raid on English soil, where do they set up their headquarters?

27. Where is Professor Browne when the Nazi soldiers' raid begins?

28. How does Miss Price fend off the German attack?

29. How are all of Miss Price's spells and witch apparatus destroyed?

30. What is Professor Browne seen doing at the film's close?

Answers on p. 247

ESCAPE TO WITCH MOUNTAIN

Released: March 1975
Running Time: 97 Minutes

The Victorian house used for the orphanage in *Escape to Witch Mountain* was long considered to be haunted by local citizenry. Located in Menlo Park, California, it was never occupied by the couple who had it built. Carmelita Coleman was killed while packing her husband's valise in preparation to move into the sixty-room mansion. A loaded gun fell from the valise and, as it hit the ground, it fired a shot, killing Carmelita.

This mansion was indeed a fitting locale for this eerie Disney offering.

Use all the psychic powers you can muster to answer the following questions.

QUESTIONS

ESCAPE TO WITCH MOUNTAIN

1. What are the names of the two psychic children around whom this movie revolves?

2. Upon their foster parents' death, where are the children taken?

3. How old were the children when their foster parents, the Malones, adopted them?

4. Aside from being able to see the future, the children are able to levitate objects. But besides that, there is something unusual about their communication with each other. What is that?

5. How does Lucas Deranian know the children have special powers?

6. What movie do all the children travel by school bus to see in this film?

7. Who plays the role of Lucas Deranian?

8. What is the name of the black cat the children own?

9. What item does one of the children always have in her possession?

10. What do the children discover about this item after it has been slightly damaged?

11. What does Lucas Deranian do to gain custody of the children?

12. For whom does Lucas Deranian work? Who plays him?

13. What is the name of the mansion to which Lucas Deranian takes the children?

14. Why does Deranian's boss want the children?

15. What are the children given as soon as they arrive at the mansion?

16. What is the name of the wild horse one of the children tames instantly?

17. One of the children can levitate at will, while the other needs the use of a certain object. What is that object?

18. When the children try to escape from the mansion, attack dogs are let loose in an effort to stop them. How do the children "handle" the dogs?

19. The next part of the children's escape is made on horseback. Eventually, they stow away in the camper of Jason O'Day. Who plays him?

20. What do the children ask Jason O'Day to do for them?

21. Deranian is hot on the trail of the children. There are two reward amounts mentioned in the film. What are they?

22. In what town are the children captured by the local sheriff?

23. Jason's brother lives just north of the city in which the children are captured. What is his name?

24. How do the children escape from jail?

25. What type of animal accompanies the children on the next leg of their journey in search of Jason's brother's home?

26. What do the townspeople proclaim upon the children's escape from jail?

27. The children finally reach the town they set out to find. What is the population of this small town?

28. What do the children finally recall about their past?

29. Who plays the role of the children's Uncle Bene in this film?

30. What do the children give Jason as remembrance for helping them return "home"?

Answers on p. 249

The Apple Dumpling Gang

Released: July 1975
Running Time: 101 Minutes

This star-studded Disney offering features a handsome gambler, a beautiful stagecoach driver, two bumbling burglars, and other assorted characters. Not to be outdone by their notable and distinguished adult counterparts, the three children featured in the film had collected some impressive credentials of their own. Clay O'Brien, who played the eldest son in the film, had already made two movies with John Wayne before *The Apple Dumpling Gang*. Brad Savage, the middle son, had thirteen commercials to his credit at the time he filmed *The Apple Dumpling Gang*. Even six-year-old Stacy Manning was already a veteran of TV commercials.

All right! Enough horsin' around! Let's get to the questions that follow!

QUESTIONS

THE APPLE DUMPLING GANG

1. In what city does this Disney film take place?

2. Why was the town named that?

3. Who plays the role of town sheriff Homer McCoy in this film?

4. What other occupations does Sheriff McCoy claim as his?

5. What two actors played the roles of bumbling criminals Theodore Ogelvie and Amos Tucker?

6. What do these two inept outlaws call themselves?

7. To what gang did Ogelvie and Tucker formerly belong, and why were they tossed out?

8. What is the name of Amos Tucker's mule?

9. The local stage coach driver is played by actress Susan Clark. What is her character's name?

10. What is the name of the stagecoach company? Who is its owner? Who played him?

11. Who played the role of Russel Donavan?

12. John Wintle asks Russel Donavan to claim "valuables" being delivered on the stage for him once he has to leave town. What do these "valuables" turn out to be?

13. Why do these "valuables" belong to John Wintle in the first place?

14. One of the stagecoach horses has bad teeth. What is his name?

15. What meal does Dusty Clydesdale bring to the Bradley children on their first night in town?

16. What mine have the Bradley children been willed by their late father?

17. On what hill is this mine located?

18. What huge item was knocked loose from the mine by an earthquake?

19. What happens to the children when this item is discovered?

20. Where is it displayed?

21. What is the name of the local café?

22. How much does a shave cost at the local barbershop?

23. If you decided to get married, how much would the justice of the peace charge to perform the ceremony?

24. The children become trapped in a runaway dumper car from which local mine?

25. When Ogelvie and Tucker attempt to steal the nugget and are caught, what is their sentence?

26. As what does outlaw Frank Stillwell pose in order to gain information on the transport of the gold nugget from the owner of the stagecoach company?

27. Which child does Stillwell take with him on his attempted escape from the bank when his heist is foiled?

28. How does Stillwell escape from the crime scene?

29. How much is the reward paid to Russel Donavan for the capture of Frank Stillwell?

30. How does Clovis Bradley respond when anyone touches him?

Answers on p. 252

PETE'S DRAGON

Released: November 1977
Running Time: 129 Minutes

This lovable musical fantasy cost Disney more than
$10,000,000 to produce. What made it different from
the other Disney films was the fact that the title char-

acter remained animated throughout the entire movie. (In the other films, the live action/animated combination was used only in individual sequences.) Elliott, the dragon, is visible on 1,770 feet of film, which translates to an incredible 28,320 individual, fully colored cels of artwork.

Stop "dragon" your heels and answer the questions that follow.

QUESTIONS

PETE'S DRAGON

1. What is Miss Taylor's occupation?

2. Who supplies the voice of Elliott?

3. Who is Nora's father, and in what building do they live?

4. What is the name of the town Pete and Elliott visit?

5. What character actor played the role of the mayor?

6. Who was responsible for the film's choreography? (Hint: She won an honorary Oscar for the choreography of *Oliver*.)

7. What fruit does Elliott eat in the beginning of the film?

8. What food delicacy does Elliott make for Pete?

9. What does Nora give Pete to eat on his arrival at the lighthouse?

10. Who is Nora's fiancée?

11. According to the song, "It's Not Easy," who are Pete's two friends?

12. Pete sleeps at Nora's lighthouse. Where does Elliott sleep?

13. Name the Tony Award-winning actor who played Dr. Terminus.

14. From where do Dr. Terminus's medicines come?

15. What is the number on Nora's lighthouse?

16. What is Lena Gogan's husband's name?

17. What does Pete catch on his boating trip with Nora and Lampie?

18. What proof do the Gogans have showing that Pete belongs to them?

19. When and where does Nora meet Elliott?

20. How much did the Gogans pay for Pete?

21. What does Nora give Elliott after he lights the lighthouse?

22. How many survivors besides Paul are there from the shipwreck?

23. Where does Paul's ship go down?

24. What is the name of the character who is the assistant to Dr. Terminus?

25. How does Nora refer to herself in this Oscar-nominated song?

Answers on p. 254

THE BLACK HOLE

Released: December 1979
Running Time: 97 Minutes

This $20,000,000 outer-space adventure introduced to the industry the most sophisticated camera system used in film at that time. It was called ACES (Automated Camera Effects System) and, according to producer Ron Miller, it allowed a great deal more flexibility in filming in miniature, as well as with all aspects of special-effects photography. Between the amazing special-effects technology and the veteran cast of actors in this film, a winning combination was guaranteed.

So get ready to blast off for an outer-space trivia adventure.

QUESTIONS

THE BLACK HOLE

1. What is the name of the spacecraft on which the cast begins their travels through space?

2. Who commands this outer-space voyage?

3. What is the name of the hovering robot computer?

4. How about this model number? (Hint: It is printed on his chest.)

5. While in outer space, our heroes come across a vessel that was recalled to Earth twenty years earlier, its mission having been labeled a failure. This ship never returned and was presumed lost or destroyed. What is the name of the spacecraft?

6. Who commands this "lost" spacecraft, and what actor portrays him?

7. When our heroes decide to board this vessel, which of the crew is told to remain behind with their ship?

8. What is unusual (and unbelievable) about the positioning of the "lost" vessel?

9. Who plays the role of Dr. Alex Durant?

10. How is Dr. Durant killed?

11. What unusual ability does crew member Kate McCrae possess?

12. Why does Kate have an acute interest in boarding the "lost" vessel, more so than any other crew member?

13. The crew happens upon a robot-computer much like their own on the vessel that they have boarded. What is this robot's name?

14. What is the name of the robot who is challenged to a futuristic game of "laser skeet shooting" by one of the hovering robot-computers?

15. The evil commander of the "lost" vessel invites our heroes to dinner on the evening they board his vessel. What are the guests served in this particular scene?

16. What do our heroes discover about the evil commander's crew (which numbered in the hundreds)?

17. One of the crew members looks to save himself when things get hairy. He sneaks back to the ship and attempts to take off, while leaving the others behind. What is this crew member's name, and what actor played the role?

18. Once their own ship has been destroyed, how do our heroes attempt to escape the black hole and its gravitational pull?

19. Why is this escape in vain?

20. How is the evil commander of the "lost" vessel killed?

Answers on p. 255

DISNEY'S THEME PARKS

Disneyland was Walt Disney's baby. He loved and nurtured it, from its beginnings on scratch paper to its actual construction. Disney spoke of Disneyland as proudly as parents speak of the first step their child has taken. The attention to detail that Walt Disney was known for in creating his films was never more evident than when he created this fantasy park ... his dream.

Since then, the dream has spread not only to the East Coast of the U.S., but overseas as well. In Japan, and soon in France, tourists from all over the globe can get a taste of the Disney magic. There's no telling where the next theme park will sprout.

This is not to say that changes aren't being planned for this country's theme parks. Included is the building of a new studio in Florida and the creation of the world's largest log-flume ride, as well as other attractions.

For a real boost, you can always count on a Disney theme park. You cannot help but leave feeling terrific—except perhaps, for tired feet.

Disneyland.

QUESTIONS

DISNEYLAND

1. When did Disneyland open?

2. What is the Fantasyland dedication?

3. What letters were given to the famous Disneyland ticket book, rating the attractions from least expensive to most expensive?

4. Where in Disneyland was Walt's apartment located?

5. What was Disneyland's biggest flop? (Hint: This was during the early years.)

6. What is the name of the steamboat considered to be "Queen of the River"?

7. What was considered Disneyland's first classic "thrill ride"?

8. What former President of the United States was on hand (along with his family) for the dedication of the Monorail on July 14, 1959?

9. On that day, what famous TV star acted as the pilot?

10. What world leader was unable to gain entrance to Disneyland, and why?

11. A petrified tree presented by Walt to his wife, Lillian, as an anniversary present in 1957, is still on display in Disneyland. Where in Disneyland is this tree located?

12. The Disney people had a name for the tree holding the Swiss Family Treehouse. What was it, and what does it mean?

13. What year did "It's a Small World" open?

14. What song do the pirates sing in The Pirates of the Caribbean?

15. What is the name of the town that is the setting for the Big Thunder Mountain Railroad climax?

16. Who played Captain EO?

17. Who produced and directed Captain EO?

18. From where did the flagpole in Town Square come?

19. How much did the base cost?
    a. $5.00
    b. $25.00
    c. $75.00

20. Along Main Street, there are large horses that pull the streetcars. What type of horses are they?

Answers on p. 261

Walt **D**isney World®

QUESTIONS

WALT DISNEY WORLD

1. When did Walt Disney World open to the general public?

2. What was the name of the first family to enter the Magic Kingdom on that day?

3. When you walk through the main entrance, on what street are you?

4. What are the names of the four steam engines of the Walt Disney World railroad?

5. This spectacular, annual summertime event made its debut in June 1977 and contains half a million twinkling lights. Can you name it?

6. At Walt Disney World we see living shrubs in the shape of animals and even Disney characters. Can you tell us what this sculpting of shrubs is called?

7. What is the tallest structure in the Magic Kingdom?

8. What is the name of the restaurant on the upper floor of Cinderella Castle?

9. What area of the Magic Kingdom is known as "The Happiest Kingdom of Them All"?

10. The following describes three attractions in the Magic Kingdom. You have probably been on them, but do you know their names?

   a. You take a scary ride through the Enchanted Forest and Diamond Mine.

   b. You take flight in a pirate galleon above the streets of London on a journey to Never Land.

   c. A wild ride along the road to "Nowhere in Particular."

11. How many horses are there on Cinderella's Golden Carrousel?

12. The attraction 20,000 Leagues Under the Sea consists of how many submarines, and what is the seating capacity for this ride?

13. The Jungle Cruise attraction was inspired by what highly acclaimed Walt Disney series?

14. Why did the original plans for Walt Disney World not include a Pirates of the Caribbean?

15. What is the storyline for Pirates of the Caribbean?

16. What could be considered the tallest mountain in Florida?

17. Name the theater that is home to Frontierland's Country Bear Jamboree.

18. How many bears make up this Jamboree? Give us the names of the two most popular stars of the show.

19. What are the dimensions of The Liberty Oak Tree, considered to be the largest living specimen in the Magic Kingdom?

20. In the Hall of Presidents, we see all the Presidents from Washington to Reagan on one stage. Which one speaks for all of them?

21. How many ghosts occupy the scary Haunted Mansion.

22. When did Space Mountain premiere at Walt Disney World, and how long did it take to complete?

23. How high does Space Mountain tower over Walt Disney World?

24. What is the Digital Animation Control System (DACS)?

25. What is the name of the Swedish-developed trash-disposal system found in Walt Disney World?

26. What is the name of the hotel in the park that is situated on the shore of Bay Lake?

27. Enclosed within this hotel's imposing steel-and-concrete A-frame is an enormous open area called what?

28. What is the uppermost floor of this hotel called? (It is where guests enjoy elegant dining, dancing, top-name entertainment, and a panoramic view of the Magic Kingdom.)

29. What is the name of the Walt Disney World mono-rail system?

30. What is the name of the lagoon that acts as an aquatic "highway," making the Magic Kingdom into a vacation kingdom?

Answers on p. 262

QUESTIONS

EPCOT CENTER

1. What does EPCOT stand for?

2. Upon entering EPCOT Center, visitors are welcomed by a million-pound sphere, considered to be the largest structure of its kind in the world. What is this sphere called, and how high is it?

3. Who are the sponsors of Spaceship Earth? Universe of Energy?

4. Where in EPCOT Center could you find a giant flying prehistoric reptile like the pteranodon?

5. What is the shape of the pavilion known as the World of Motion?

6. In the World of Motion, guests enjoy an amusing vauderville show entitled "The Bird and the Robot." What is the name given to the robot?

7. Who are our hosts through the World of Imagination?

8. Of all the pavilions in EPCOT Center, which is the largest?

9. What is the name of the show that focuses on nutrition through the use of talking broccoli, talking bread, and examples of many other food groups?

10. What is Communicore?

11. Name the sponsors of the following exhibits:
    a. Energy Exchange
    b. Future Com
    c. TravelPort

12. The American Adventure is a dramatic trip through this country's history. What two famous Americans host this adventure?

13. Where does the American Adventure end?

14. What are the two major areas of EPCOT Center?

Answers on p. 265

ANSWERS
DISNEY'S
ANIMATED
CLASSICS

SNOW WHITE AND THE SEVEN DWARFS

1. She is singing "I'm Wishing."

2. The heart he brings to the queen comes from a pig.

3. We first encounter the dwarfs working in their diamond mine.

4. The dwarfs are famous for "Heigh Ho."

5. The dwarfs are alerted to the fact that Snow White is in danger by the animals in the forest.

6. The forest animals help Snow White with the cleaning as she sings "Whistle While You Work."

7. She is obsessed with her own beauty.

8. They were Doc, Dopey, Grumpy, Happy, Sleepy, Bashful, and Sneezy.

9. Snow White's voice was supplied by 19-year-old Adriana Caselotti.

10. Dopey is the only one without a beard.

11. Dopey has one tooth.

12. "She's a female, and all females are poison!"

13. The only thing that can save Snow White is "Love's First Kiss."

14. Doc is considered the leader of the Dwarfs.

15. "Mummy dust to make me old.
   To shroud my clothes the black of night
   To age my voice an old hag's cackle
   To whiten my hair—a scream of fright
   A blast of wind to fan my hate
   A thunderbolt to mix it well"

16. We see the prince early in the film when he sings with Snow White, and at the end of the film when his kiss wakes her up.

17. It consisted of eight Oscars: one full-sized one and seven miniature ones, all on the same base (the award was presented to Walt by Shirley Temple).

18. When Snow White is visited by the wicked queen, she is busy making a gooseberry pie for the Seven Dwarfs.

19. She tells her it is a magic wishing apple ... one bite and all Snow White's dreams will come true.

20. Her coffin is made of glass and gold.

PINOCCHIO

1. The story of Pinocchio was written by Collodi (Carlo Lorenzini).

2. The Oscar-winning song is titled "When You Wish Upon a Star."

3. The wood carver's name is Geppetto.

4. The kitten's name is Figaro, and the fish is Cleo.

5. The whale's name is Monstro.

6. Pinocchio's nose grows when he tells a lie.

7. Jiminy Cricket carries an umbrella.

8. Geppetto notices a wishing star.

9. His wish is for Pinocchio to become a real boy, and it is granted by the Blue Fairy.

10. Pinocchio is made of pine wood.

11. He has to prove himself brave, truthful, and unselfish.

12. Jiminy Cricket serves as Pinocchio's "conscience."

13. "Give a little whistle and always let your conscience be your guide" is the advice Jiminy gives him.

14. He sleeps in a matchbox.

15. Stromboli is famous for marionette shows.

16. Pinocchio is sold to Stromboli by Honest John, (aka J. Worthington Foulfellow) and Stromboli keeps him in a bird cage.

17. Honest John sings the song.

18. They never return from Pleasure Island.

19. The boys are turned into donkeys.

20. Pinocchio eats pie and ice cream.

21. A message floats down from a dove sent by the Blue Fairy.

22. Pinocchio builds a fire and when Monstro sneezes, they escape.

23. The Blue Fairy turns Pinocchio into a real boy.

24. He is given an 18-karat gold "Official Conscience" medal.

25. Pinocchio saves Geppetto from death.

FANTASIA

1. The soundtrack of *Fantasia* was the first ever recorded in stereophonic sound (called "Fantasound" by Disney).

2. The orchestra was conducted by the great Leopold Stokowski.

3. We see the silhouettes of the musicians, and of Stokowski as he begins conducting the "concert."

4. Prominently featured in the opening segment are violinists, cellists, French-horn players, and a harpist.

5. Dewdrop Fairies perform the "Dance of the Sugar Plum Fairies."

6. In the "Chinese Dance," Hop Low and his mushroom buddies are the performers.

7. "The Dance of the Reed Flutes" is performed by flowers on the water's surface.

8. The "Arabian Dance" sequence takes place underwater.

9. The Cossack-like thistles dance the "Russian Dance."

10. "The Waltz of the Flowers" features the Autumn Fairies, the Frost Fairies, and the Snowflake Fairies.

11. Mickey Mouse stars in "The Sorcerer's Apprentice" sequence.

12. The Sorcerer's Apprentice borrows the Sorcerer's hat.

13. Mickey turns a broom into his personal servant to fetch water; it gets out of control and multiplies, causing the well to overflow and flood the Sorcerer's chambers.

14. Disney used the "Rite of Spring" scene to present a panorama of the theory of evolution.

15. The opening sequence, "Trip Through Space," is a journey from deep space to Earth.

16. "Fight" features a battle between a stegosaurus and a Tyrannosaurus Rex. (The Tyrannosaurus wins.)

17. "The Pastoral Symphony" takes place in ancient Greece.

18. The Mount Olympus sequence features Pegasus and his family.

19. Bacchus's donkey-unicorn is Jacchus.

20. Zeus hurls lightning bolts at Bacchus in "The Storm."

21. Ostriches, Hippos, Elephants, and Alligators are featured in "Dance of the Hours."

22. Bald Mountain (actually Mount Triglat) is near Kiev, Russia.

23. On Bald Mountain, the evil spirits gather on Walpurgis Night.

24. The Devil is Chernobog.

25. The bells also call the faithful to worship.

DUMBO

1. Dumbo's mother's name is Mrs. Jumbo.

2. The circus winter quarters are located in Florida.

3. Dumbo's large ears unfurl when he sneezes.

4. She is riding Casey, Jr.

5. Sterling Holloway was the voice of the messenger stork.

6. Dumbo is given the name of "Jumbo, Jr."

7. The other elephants in the cage with Mrs. Jumbo give Dumbo his more popular name.

8. The mouse's name is Timothy.

9. The elephants are frightened by Timothy, the mouse.

10. The "joke" is that when Dumbo plunges from a burning building into the safety net, he goes straight through to land in a vat of plaster.

11. The song is called "We're Gonna Hit the Big Boss for a Raise."

12. Dumbo imagined a great pageant of dancing, trumpeting pink elephants.

13. The five crows give Dumbo a "magic feather," with which he thinks he can fly.

14. The song is "When I See an Elephant Fly."

15. Dumbo's ears are insured for $1,000,000.

BAMBI

1. The news of Bambi's birth is heralded by a rabbit named Thumper.

2. Thumper teaches Bambi to talk.

3. Having just learned the word "flower," Bambi calls the skunk by that name. The skunk is embarrassed but pleased, noting "He can call me Flower if he wants to."

4. Bambi falls for a real dear named Faline.

5. Bambi's father is referred to as The Great Prince of the Forest.

6. Thumper teaches Bambi how to skate on "stiff water."

7. Bambi's mother is shot by hunters.

8. The owl is referred to as Friend Owl.

9. A buck called Ronno challenges Bambi for his lady's favors.

10. Faline is being threatened by a pack of vicious hunting dogs.

11. Bambi is shot by hunters (but survives).

12. Faline's mother is Aunt Ena.

13. Faline gives birth to two fawns.

14. His father simply states, "Man was in the forest."

15. The owl says when they feel like that, they're "twitterpated."

16. (You're going to hate us for this one!) Thumper's mother is, simply, Mrs. Rabbit.

17. By film's end, Bambi is recognized as the new Great Prince of the Forest.

18. The first word Bambi speaks is "bur-dah," or "bird."

SONG OF THE SOUTH

1. Uncle Remus is played by actor James Baskett.

2. Johnny's father is a journalist off on assignment.

3. Johnny misses his father terribly and wants to run away to join him.

4. The song "Zip-a-dee-Doo-Dah" won an Academy Award. It was written by Allie Wrubel and Ray Gilbert.

5. Johnny's mother is played by veteran actress Ruth Warrick.

6. Brer Rabbit found himself hung upside down from a tree—the result of a trap set by his enemy.

7. Brer Rabbit coaxes Brer Bear to take his place in the trap by telling him he is "makin' a dollar a minute" hanging there.

8. Brer Rabbit's main antagonist in all these tales is Brer Fox.

9. You can't run away from trouble because "dey ain't no place dat fur."

10. Ginny Favers gives Johnny the puppy to protect it from her mean brothers.

11. Ginny's brothers lie about Johnny's stealing the puppy, because they resent his having it.

12. As he strolls through the woods, in the story, Brer Rabbit is greeted by Brer Frog, Brer Possum, and Brer Fish.

13. The Tar Baby does not return Brer Rabbit's greeting, no matter how many times Brer Rabbit says hello.

14. The Tar Baby is a trap to lure Brer Rabbit into trying to fight it. Upon throwing a punch, the rabbit's paw gets stuck on the tar creature and unable to escape, he becomes easy prey for Brer Fox.

15. The title of this third tale is "The Laughing Place."

16. Brer Rabbit leads Brer Bear and Brer Fox to a swarming beehive and they become suddenly preoccupied with their own problems, allowing Brer Rabbit to escape.

17. Mr. Bluebird (as in "Mr. Bluebird on my shoulder") appears in the final sequence of the film.

18. The group is joined by another friend named Toby.

19. The Uncle Remus stories were written by Joel Chandler Harris.

20. The voice of Brer Fox is provided by none other than James Baskett, who also plays Uncle Remus in the film.

CINDERELLA

1. Ilene Woods was the voice of Cinderella.

2. Lucifer the Cat is the only animal that was hostile toward Cinderella.

3. Lady Tremaine is Cinderella's stepmother.

4. The stepmother treats Cinderella as a servant.

5. Her stepsisters are Anastasia and Drizella.

6. The two most notable mice are Gus and Jaq.

7. Gus is saved by Cinderella.

8. He is worried about how the royal line will continue, since his only son is not married.

9. Every eligible maiden in the land will be invited.

10. If Cinderella gets all her work done and can find something presentable to wear, her stepmother will let her attend the ball.

11. Cinderella's stepmother plays the piano.

12. Cinderella's fairy godmother has no name.

13. She wears a blue gown.

14. She says *"Bibbidi-Bobbidi-Boo."*

15. She turns a pumpkin into a coach.

16. The coachman was a horse.
    The footman was a dog.
    The horses were the mice.

17. The spell expires at the last stroke of midnight.

18. They sing "So This Is Love."

19. She wears glass slippers.

20. Gus, Jaq, and Bruno the dog help her escape from the tower room.

ALICE IN WONDERLAND

1. Alice's sister is reading a history lesson to her.

2. Alice's kitten is named Dinah.

3. Alice is looking into a reflecting pool when her unbelievable adventure begins.

4. Alice first sees the White Rabbit, who is lamenting the fact that he is "late for a very important date."

5. Alice is advised to drink the potion by the door-knob on the door that she cannot fit through.

6. Alice describes the taste of the potion first as cherry tarts, then custard, pineapple, and, finally, roast turkey.

7. After shrinking to a tiny size, Alice eats a wafer and becomes a giant. Her tears flood the room and after once again drinking the potion she shrinks back to a tiny size, and floats through the keyhole in the now-empty bottle.

8. Alice, still in her glass bottle, passes the Dodo, a bird, on the high seas.

9. Upon being drawn into the forest by the White Rabbit, Alice meets Tweedledum and Tweedledee.

10. Tweedledum and Tweedledee tell Alice the story of "The Walrus and the Carpenter."

11. Baby oysters—coaxed out of their sea bed by the Walrus, they become his dinner.

12. The White Rabbit (thinking she is his servant), calls Alice "Mary Ann."

13. The White Rabbit and the Dodo refer to her as "the monster."

14. The services of Bill, a lizard with a ladder, are enlisted in an attempt to pull Alice through the chimney of the house she now occupies completely.

15. In order to shrink, Alice eats a carrot from the White Rabbit's garden.

16. Alice meets several bread-and-butterflies and a rocking horse fly.

17. The talking flowers sing a song for Alice entitled "All in a Golden Afternoon."

18. The flowers come to the conclusion that Alice is a weed.

19. The "smoke-ring-letter-blowing" insect is a caterpillar.

20. The vegetable with the power to make Alice shrink or grow is a mushroom.

21. Alice meets the Cheshire Cat, perhaps the strangest character in the film.

22. The Mad Hatter and the March Hare are in the midst of a tea party, singing "A Very Merry Un-Birthday to You."

23. The card attached to the Mad Hatter's hat reads "10/6."

24. The dormouse can only be calmed, Alice is advised, by rubbing jam on his nose.

25. The Mad Hatter asks Alice why a raven is like a writing desk.

26. The sign reads "Tulgey Wood."

27. The Cheshire Cat shows Alice a shortcut.

28. Alice first meets up with the ace, two, and three of clubs, who are busily painting all the white roses in the kingdom red.

29. Upon finding Alice guilty, the Queen sentences Alice to be beheaded.

30. These following actors provided the voices for the characters as follows:
    a. Alice—Kathryn Beaumont
    b. Cheshire Cat—Sterling Holloway
    c. Mad Hatter—Ed Wynn
    d. March Hare—Jerry Colonna

PETER PAN

1. *Peter Pan* is based on the play *Peter Pan* by Sir James M. Barrie.

2. Peter Pan searches for his shadow.

3. The story takes place in London.

4. Their first names are George and Mary. Mary Darling actually thought Peter Pan was the Spirit of Youth.

5. They have three children: John, Michael, and Wendy.

6. Peter Pan's companion is Tinker Bell, a pixie.

7. They have a nursemaid named Nana, who is a dog (a Saint Bernard).

8. Never Land is a place where children go who don't want to grow up.

9. The only way to get to Never Land is to fly.

10. According to Peter Pan, Never Land is located past the second star to the right and straight on till morning.

11. The pirate captain is Captain Hook.

12. Captain Hook's sidekick is Mr. Smee.

13. Captain Hook has a hook where his left hand used to be. As the story goes, Peter Pan caused Captain Hook to lose his hand.

14. The crocodile ate Captain Hook's hand and, since it tasted so good, he wants more of the captain.

15. He hears the ticking of a clock that the crocodile swallowed.

16. Tiger Lily is the kidnapped Indian princess.

17. Captain Hook takes her to Skull Rock.

18. Hangman's Tree is the entrance to Peter Pan's hideaway.

19. Peter Pan's nickname for Captain Hook is "Cod Fish."

20. They sprinkle pixie dust on Hook's ship and fly home.

LADY AND THE TRAMP

1. Peggy Lee and Sonny Burke wrote the songs for *Lady and the Tramp.*

2. Money cannot buy the wag of a dog's tail.

3. The story opens and ends at Christmastime.

4. Jim Dear and Darling are Lady's owners.

5. Lady always accidentally tears a hole in the paper's front page—which makes the world seem a much happier place to Jim Dear.

6. Lady received her dog license at the age of six months.

7. Lady's collar is blue.

8. Jock wears the plaid sweater. His companion is Trusty.

9. Trusty's grandpappy's name is Old Reliable.

10. The Italian Restaurant is Tony's.

11. The two words are "That Dog."

12. The baby is born in April.

13. Jim Dear goes out for watermelon and chop suey.

14. Aunt Sarah comes to watch the baby.

15. Lady is a cocker spaniel, and Tramp a mutt.

16. Aunt Sarah brings Siamese cats.

17. The names of her cats are Si and Am.

18. Aunt Sarah buys a muzzle.

19. Tramp rescues Lady.

20. They go the zoo, where a beaver takes Lady's muzzle off.

21. The sign reads "No Dogs Allowed."

22. Joe serves Lady and Tramp spaghetti and meatballs.

23. Tramp calls "Lady Pidge," for "Pigeon."

24. The dogs in the pound call Lady "Miss Park Avenue."

25. She sings "He's a Tramp."

26. A dog license is a passport to freedom.

27. Lady and the Tramp have four puppies.

28. They have three cockers and one tramp.

29. The dogcatcher's van overturns onto Trusty, but Trusty escapes with a broken leg.

30. Aunt Sarah sends the dogs biscuits for Christmas.

SLEEPING BEAUTY

1. The princess's name at birth was Aurora.

2. She was named after the dawn because she filled her parents' lives with sunshine.

3. The names of the three fairies are Flora, Fauna, and Merryweather.

4. King Stefan is Aurora's father, and King Hubert is Prince Phillip's father.

5. The intention is to unite their kingdoms.

6. The princess is betrothed to Prince Phillip.

7. The evil fairy Maleficent prophesies that before sunset on the princess's sixteenth birthday, Aurora will prick her finger on the spindle of a spinning wheel and die.

8. Maleficent knows nothing about love, kindness, and the joy of helping others.

9. The fairies dress as peasant women and raise Aurora in the forest.

10. Maleficent lives in the Forbidden Mountain.

11. Aurora has lips as red as a rose.

12. The good fairies raise Aurora in a woodcutter's cottage in the forest.

13. The fairies call Aurora "Briar Rose."

14. Fauna makes Aurora's birthday cake.

15. Prince Phillip's horse is named Samson.

16. They sing "Once Upon a Dream."

17. *Sleeping Beauty* takes place in the fourteenth century.

18. They put the whole kingdom to sleep until Aurora awakens.

19. The song likens Aurora's hair to golden sunshine.

20. The weapons are a shield of virtue and the sword of truth.

21. She turns into a fire-breathing dragon.

22. She turns it into stone.

23. Maleficent puts a forest of thorns around King Stefan's castle.

24. He throws the sword of truth into its heart.

ONE HUNDRED AND ONE DALMATIANS

1. Pongo's owner is songwriter Roger Radcliff.

2. The Dalmatian Pongo is determined to meet is named Perdita.

3. Roger, and Perdita's owner, Anita, end up in a pond as the dogs frolic. They later marry.

4. Perdita gives birth to fifteen puppies, including one thought stillborn that Roger saves.

5. Nanny, Roger Radcliff's servant, acts as midwife during the birth.

6. Cruella De Vil offers to buy the puppies. She wants to make a fur coat out of them.

7. Cruella hires Jasper and Horace Badun to dognap the pups.

8. Pongo and Perdita use the "Twilight Bark" to learn the whereabouts of the pups.

9. The puppies are at Hell Hall, Cruella's house in Suffolk.

10. Pongo and Perdita are aided in the rescue by Sergeant Tibs (a cat), the Captain (a horse), and the Colonel (a sheepdog).

11. Cruella De Vil is holding captive a total of ninety-nine puppies.

12. The Dalmatians cover themselves with soot so they resemble black Labradors.

13. The troupe is aided by a collie and a Labrador.

14. This adventure takes place in England.

15. The dogs look like their owners—or vice versa.

16. The most prominent of Perdita's pups are Rolly, Lucky, Freckles, Pepper, Patch, and Penny.

17. The cows are named Queenie, Princess, and Duchess.

18. The parody of "What's My Line" is "What's My Crime?"

19. Percival Fauncewater, an old mate of the Baduns, is the featured criminal.

20. Thunderbolt's adversary is Dirty Dawson.

THE SWORD IN THE STONE

1. The film is based on the book of the same name, written by T. H. White.

2. The wizard's name is Merlin.

3. The wizard's familiar is an owl named Archimedes.

4. His name is Arthur, but his nickname is Wart.

5. His foster father is Sir Ector.

6. He falls through Merlin's roof while looking for an arrow.

7. The winner of the tournament will be crowned King of all England.

8. The sword is stuck through an anvil on a stone, in the center of a courtyard.

9. "Who so pulleth out this sword of this stone and anvil is rightwise King born of England."

10. The boy wants to be a fish.

11. Merlin turns Wart into a squirrel and also a bird.

12. Her name is Mad Madam Mim.

13. Archimedes the owl teaches the boy.

14. She turns herself into a cat while the boy is still a bird.

15. In a wizard's duel, the wizards try to destroy each other by turning themselves into different creatures.

16. The four rules are as follows:
    a. can only change into animals
    b. no make-believe creatures (for example, no pink dragons)
    c. cannot become invisible
    d. no cheating

17. He turns himself into a germ for a rare disease and Mim catches it.

18. She hates sunshine.

19. The young boy who becomes known as King Arthur.

20. Knowledge and wisdom are the real powers that get you through life.

THE JUNGLE BOOK

1. Mowgli is found by a panther named Bagheera, who remains his guardian throughout the film.

2. Mowgli's wolf father is called Rama.

3. The tiger Shere Khan desires Mowgli for his next meal.

4. Akela leads the wolf pack. The pack decides that Mowgli should be returned to a human village for his own safety.

5. Mowgli and Bagheera meet up with the hypnotic Kaa, a boa constrictor who also desires a human meal.

6. The elephant herd is led by Colonel Hathi, also an elephant.

7. Colonel Hathi's wife is Winifred.

8. Mowgli meets and makes friends with the amiable Baloo, a bear.

9. Bagheera considers Baloo a "jungle bum."

10. A band of apes and monkeys captures Mowgli.

11. The leader of the monkeys and apes is King Louie, an orangutan.

12. King Louie wants Mowgli to teach him the "secret" of making fire.

13. King Louie wants to be more like man, and sings "I Wanna Be Like You."

14. Bagheera enlists the aid of Colonel Hathi and his elephant troop.

15. The four vultures are named Buzzie, Dizzy, Ziggy, and Flaps.

16. Baloo is apparently slain by Shere Khan, the tiger.

17. Shere Khan is deathly afraid of fire, which is how Mowgli escapes his clutches with help from the four vultures.

18. Mowgli sees a little girl, and is smitten by her beauty and her mysterious song.

19. Baloo warns: "Forget about those—they ain't nothin' but trouble!"

20. The cast performs "The Bare Necessities" as the film ends.

THE ARISTOCATS

1. Duchess's owner is Madame Adelaide Bonfamille.

2. Duchess's kittens are named Toulouse, Berlioz, and Marie.

3. Madame Bonfamille's lawyer is M. Georges Hautecourt.

4. The money would go to the thieving butler Edgar.

5. Edgar drugs the cats' food with sleeping pills.

6. The house mouse in this film is a good friend to the cats. His name is Roquefort.

7. Two dogs named Lafayette and Napoleon attack Edgar and ruin his plan.

8. The drowsy cats are helped by amiable Thomas O'Malley, an alley cat.

9. The cats want to get back to Paris, and Madame Bonfamille.

10. Frou Frou, a horse, encourages Roquefort to search for his cat friends.

11. Abigail and Amelia Gabble save Thomas O'Malley from drowning.

12. The Gabble geese are traveling to Paris to visit their Uncle Waldo.

13. The cats stow away in a milk truck.

14. The cat band entertains the cats with a song called "Ev'rybody Wants to Be a Cat."

15. The leader of the cat band is Scat Cat.

16. Edgar puts the cats in a trunk marked for delivery to Timbuktu.

17. Roquefort picks the trunk's lock with his tail and frees the cats.

18. Madame Bonfamille decides to turn her home into a foundation for all the alley cats of Paris.

19. Duchess plays the harp.

20. The voice of Duchess is provided by Eva Gabor.

ROBIN HOOD

1. The following characters are represented by the following animals:
   a. Prince John—a lion.
   b. Friar Tuck—a badger.
   c. Little John—a bear.
   d. Robin Hood—a fox.
   e. The Sheriff of Nottingham—a wolf.

2. Voices for the characters were provided by the following:
   a. The Rooster—singer Roger Miller.
   b. Little John—comedian Phil Harris.
   c. Sir Hiss—British actor Terry-Thomas.
   d. Prince John—Peter Ustinov.
   e. Friar Tuck—Andy Devine.

3. Little John most often refers to Robin Hood as "Rob."

4. Prince John usurps the crown after King Richard goes off on a great crusade to the Holy Land.

5. King Richard leaves on the crusade only after Sir Hiss hypnotizes him into doing so.

6. The royal coach is pulled by elephants. They also act as trumpeters for the procession.

7. Prince John's "henchmen" are, in fact, "hench-rhinos."

8. The prince is traveling to Nottingham via the King's Highway.

9. Robin Hood and Little John pose as female fortune tellers.

10. Prince John sucks his thumb in a display of infantile insecurity.

11. "The Phony King of England" was written by Johnny Mercer.

12. The posters displayed on trees in Sherwood Forest promised one thousand pounds to anyone who could capture the "outlaw" Robin Hood.

13. The village blacksmith is Otto, a hound dog.

14. Skippy is seven.

15. Robin Hood presents Skippy with not only a bow and arrow, but his very own hat, as well.

16. Robin Hood disguises himself as an old, blind beggar.

17. Skippy's turtle pal is named Toby.

18. Toby and Skippy play at being Robin Hood, of course.

19. Skippy finds Maid Marian and Lady Kluck playing badminton.

20. The picture Maid Marian keèps of childhood sweetheart Robin Hood is, in fact, a "Wanted" poster.

21. The winner is to receive a golden arrow and a kiss from the fair Maid Marian.

22. Robin Hood enters the contest disguised as a stork from Devonshire.

23. Little John poses as Sir Reginald, Duke of Chutney, at the tournament.

24. Robin Hood and the Sheriff of Nottingham are the tournament finalists.

25. The church organ is played by a church mouse.

26. Friar Tuck is arrested for "high treason to the Crown" (he tries to prevent the Sheriff from taking the money in the church's poor box).

27. Prince John tries to set a trap for Robin Hood by hanging Friar Tuck. He anticipates that Robin Hood will attempt to rescue his friend.

28. Trigger and Nutsy, palace guards, are vultures. George Lindsey provided Trigger's voice, and Ken Curtis Nutsy's.

29. Trigger calls his crossbow "Old Betsy."

30. As the film closes, Robin Hood and Maid Marian have just wed and are seen leaving Nottingham by coach to begin their honeymoon.

THE RESCUERS

1. Penny sends her message in a bottle.

2. Penny's message is found by two beachcombers, who happen to be mice. They find the message when it floats into New York Harbor.

3. The mice take the message to the International Rescue Aid Society.

4. Bianca chooses Bernard, a janitor, as her partner in her attempt to find Penny.

5. Penny's message directs our sleuths to the Morningside Orphanage in New York.

6. Upon arriving at the orphanage, they meet Rufus, a cat, who suspects that Penny has run away.

7. Madame Medusa is said to have been seen with Penny on the day she disappeared.

8. The evil woman owns Madame Medusa's Pawn Shop Boutique.

9. Penny is on a houseboat on Devil's Bayou.

10. In order to reach Devil's Bayou, Bianca and her partner travel aboard Orville, an albatross. Orville works for the Albatross Air Charter Service.

11. Upon reaching their destination, our sleuths are aided by two muskrats named Ellie Mae and Luke.

12. They are Nero and Brutus.

13. Madame Medusa is assisted by the bumbling Mr. Snoops.

14. They use her to fit through a cave's narrow opening and recover a valuable gem.

15. The helpful dragonfly's name is Evinrude.

16. Madame Medusa goes after a brilliant diamond called the Devil's Eye.

17. The valuable diamond is hidden in Penny's teddy bear.

18. Penny and the others escape using Madame Medusa's jet-powered swampmobile.

19. Penny donates what is recognized as the world's largest diamond to a museum.

20. The International Rescue Aid Society is located in the basement of the United Nations.

THE FOX AND THE HOUND

1. An owl called Big Mama finds the fox cub.

2. Big Mama takes the fox cub to the home of Widow Tweed in the hopes that she will adopt him.

3. Dinky the sparrow and Boomer the woodpecker assist Big Mama in transporting the fox cub.

4. Widow Tweed calls him Tod, because he is reminiscent of a toddler.

5. The hunter's name is Amos Slade.

6. Amos's two dogs are Chief and Copper.

7. Copper, who is only a puppy, becomes Tod's best pal after one day of play.

8. Widow Tweed is forced to keep Tod indoors because Chief, the hunting dog, is determined to catch him.

9. After several more dangerous encounters, Widow Tweed takes Tod to a game preserve for his protection.

10. The voice for Big Mama is provided by Pearl Bailey.

11. Tod falls head over hoof for a lovely young vixen named Vixey. Vixey's voice is provided by Sandy Duncan.

12. In order to impress Vixey, Todd attempts to catch a fish.

13. Amos Slade gets caught in one of his own traps while retreating from a bear.

14. Tod diverts the bear's attention and Amos is able to free himself.

15. Amos Slade's voice is provided by Jack Albertson.

16. Widow Tweed sings "Good-bye May Seem Forever."

17. Widow Tweed's old cow is named Abigail.

18. The caterpillar is called Squeeks.

19. The voice of Copper is provided by Disney favorite Kurt Russell.

20. Tod's voice, as an adult fox, was provided by film veteran Mickey Rooney.

THE BLACK CAULDRON

1. The film takes place in Prydain, a kingdom in Wales.

2. Whoever possessed the black cauldron could command a legion of invincible warriors called the Cauldron Born. These warriors enabled their master to rule all.

3. Taran lives with the old wizard Dallben in Caer Dallben.

4. Taran is Assistant Pig Keeper. He takes care of a pig called Hen Wen.

5. Taran longs to fight against the evil Horned King.

6. The King seeks the black cauldron and he knows that Hen Wen's psychic powers can lead him to his treasure.

7. Upon awakening, Taran meets Gurgi, a hairy little creature.

8. Hen Wen is being chased by gwythaints—a mixture of vulture and pterodactyl.

9. Creeper threatens to execute Hen Wen.

10. He is abducted and thrown into an underground dungeon.

11. Taran meets the beautiful princess Eilonwy, who is also a prisoner of the evil king.

12. Taran takes the sword from the burial place of a past castle inhabitant.

13. Taran and Eilonwy rescue Fflewddur Fflam, a minstrel.

14. The king of the Fair Folk is Eidilleg.

15. The king tells all that the cauldron is hidden in the marshes of Morva.

16. The three witches of Morva are Orgoch, Orddu, and Orwen.

17. The witches want Taran's sword, which has magic powers.

18. Gurgi flings himself into the cauldron.

19. The evil Horned King is sucked into the black cauldron and perishes.

20. Taran trades the cauldron for the return of Gurgi.

THE GREAT MOUSE DETECTIVE

1. Our story begins on the eve of Queen Moustoria's Diamond Jubilee, as well as on Olivia Flaversham's birthday.

2. Olivia's father's name is Hiram, and he is a toy maker.

3. Fidget, a bat, kidnaps Hiram and brings him to the evil Ratigan. There, Hiram is told to make a lifelike robot of the queen.

4. Ratigan's voice is provided by horror film legend Vincent Price.

5. Olivia is discovered by Dr. David Q. Dawson.

6, Olivia is seeking the great Basil to help find her father.

7. Basil lives in the basement of 221B Baker Street— right beneath another famous detective, Sherlock Holmes.

8. Basil's housekeeper is Mrs. Judson.

9. He wants to be crowned King Ratigan I.

10. Toby, a loyal bloodhound, helps Basil find his quarry.

11. Olivia is in a toy store.

12. The piece of paper is traced to "The Rat Trap."

13. The good doctor dances with a mouse chorus line.

14. Basil and Dr. Dawson are tied to a mousetrap that is geared to execute them several different ways simultaneously.

15. It is not the queen at all. It is the robot replica that Hiram Flaversham was forced to build against his will.

16. Ratigan and Fidget escape in a dirigible.

17. Ratigan crashes into the clock atop the Houses of Parliament. (The clock tower is the famous "Big Ben.")

18. Basil was named after Basil Rathbone, the actor who played Sherlock Holmes in the movies for many years.

19. Ratigan's pet is a fat pink cat named Felicia.

20. The juggler is, of course, an octupus.

ANSWERS
DISNEY ON
TELEVISION

WALT DISNEY PRESENTS—MATCHING ANSWERS

1. i
2. e
3. a
4. h
5. g
6. b

7. k
8. c
9. d
10. j
11. f

WALT DISNEY'S WONDERFUL WORLD OF COLOR —MATCHING ANSWERS

1. i
2. f or i
3. b
4. g
5. a
6. d

7. l
8. j
9. c
10. h
11. e
12. k

THE WONDERFUL WORLD OF DISNEY— MATCHING ANSWERS

1. e
2. k
3. g

4. c
5. h
6. a

DAVY CROCKETT

1. Fess Parker plays Davy Crockett.

2. Buddy Ebsen plays George Russel, Davy Crockett's old-time friend.

3. General Andrew Jackson (Basil Ruysdael) asks Davy for help in defeating a band of Indians.

4. The name of the Indian chief, as played by Pat Hogan, is Chief Red Stick.

5. He uses the victory to win the Indian chief's friendship. Davy persuades Red Stick to sign a peace treaty.

6. We learn of Davy Crockett's wife's death in "Davy Crockett Goes to Congress."

7. Davy's adversary in the riverboat race is Mike Fink.

8. His motto is: "Be sure you're right; then go ahead."

9. Kenneth Tobey plays Colonel Jim Bowie.

10. Davy Crockett calls his rifle his "Old Betsy."

1. Roy Williams is known as the Big Mooseketeer.

2. The head Mouseketeer is Jimmie Dodd.

3. The selection of Mouseketeers was made by "Jimmie Dodd, Roy Williams, Bill Walsh, and Walt himself.

4. Mouseketeers were paid $185 per week to start.

5. Jimmie Dodd wrote "The Mickey Mouse March."

6. Monday . . . . Fun with Music Day
   Tuesday . . . . Guest Star Day
   Wednesday . . . . Anything Can Happen Day
   Thursday . . . . Circus Day
   Friday . . . . Talent Roundup Day

7. The original nine were:

Sharon Baird	Darlene Gillespie
Bobby Burgess	Carl "Cubby" O'Brien
Lonnie Burr	Karen Pendleton
Tommy Cole	Doreen Tracey
Annette Funicello	

8. The "Hardy Boys" were played by Tommy Kirk and Tim Considine.

9. Spin was played by Tim Considine, and Marty was played by David Stollery.

10. Marty's real name is Martin Markham.

11. The name of the camp in the Spin and Marty series is the Triple R Ranch.

12. Marty conquers his fear of horses by learning to ride Skyrocket.

13. The sequel to "Spin and Marty" included Annette Funicello and Darlene Gillespie.

14. Moochie was played by Kevin Corcoran.

15. a) Johnny Crawford played Chuck Connors's son in "The Rifleman."
    b) Tim Considine starred in "My Three Sons," as well as in *The Shaggy Dog*.
    c) Bobby Burgess was a regular on "The Lawrence Welk Show."
    d) Carl "Cubby" O'Brien was an orchestra member on "The Carol Burnett Show."
    e) Paul Petersen played Jeff Stone on "The Donna Reed Show."

ZORRO (1957—1959 ON ABC).

1. Zorro is played by the handsome Guy Williams.

2. Zorro's real name is Don Diego de la Vega.

3. This series is set in 1820.

4. The setting for this series is Spanish California (Los Angeles).

5. Zorro is studying in Spain before returning home.

6. Zorro's father, Don Alejandro, is played by George J. Lewis.

7. Captain Monastario (Britt Lomond) is the wicked commandant who has taken over the Fortress de los Angeles and is tormenting its citizenry.

8. Captain Monastario's underling is Sergeant Garcia, as played by Henry Calvin.

9. Zorro's sidekick is the loyal and trustworthy Bernardo. Bernardo is played by actor Gene Sheldon.

10. Zorro is famous for the "Z" he cuts with his sword.

11. Zorro's love interest was a character named Anna Maria Verdugo, played by Jolene Brand.

12. Zorro's horses are named Tornado and Phantom.

13. Annette Funicello plays the role of Anita Cabrillo.

14. The theme song used for this series is aptly named "Theme from Zorro."

15. The hit single of "Theme from Zorro" was recorded by the popular group The Chordettes.

MICKEY MOUSE

1. Mickey's first film was *Steamboat Willie* (1928).

2. Mickey becomes an aviator in *Plane Crazy* (1928).

3. Mickey runs into trouble when he attempts to duplicate Donald Duck over and over again.

4. Mickey tries to take Pluto along.

5. Mickey is a humble hero in *Brave Little Tailor* (1938).

6. The first Mickey Mouse film shot in Technicolor was *The Band Concert* (1935).

7. *Orphan's* (sic) *Benefit* was made in 1934 and 1941.

8. *Thru the Mirror* is based on *Through the Looking-Glass (Alice in Wonderland)*.

9. Mickey brilliantly plays the role of the Sorcerer's Apprentice in *Fantasia*.

10. Mickey hit the charts in a big way with *Mickey Mouse Disco*.

11. Mickey first speaks in *The Karnival Kid* (1929).

12. *Lend a Paw* is a remake of *Mickey's Pal Pluto* (1933).

13. Mickey is a gridiron star in *Touchdown Mickey* (1932).

14. Mickey finds a bunch of kittens on his doorstep.

15. Mickey has a great deal of trouble getting an inner tube back into a tire.

16. Mickey proves victorious over Mortimer Mouse.

17. Mickey and Pluto first appear together in *The Chain Gang* (1930).

18. Chip and Dale decide to live in Pluto's Christmas tree.

19. Mickey returned to the big screen in *Mickey's Christmas Carol*.

20. Mickey plays the role of Bob Cratchit.

DONALD DUCK

1. Donald's first film is *The Wise Little Hen* (1934).

2. Donald recites "Mary Had a Little Lamb" and "Little Boy Blue."

3. Donald's love interest is Donna Duck. The character later became Daisy Duck.

4. Donald appears as a solo star for the first time in *Modern Inventions* (1937).

5. *Donald's Decision* asks the audience to buy Canadian War Bonds.

6. Folks are asked to file taxes in *The New Spirit* (1942). The message is repeated a year later in *The Spirit of '43*.

7. The 1943 Academy Award for Best Cartoon Short Subject went to *Der Fuehrer's Face*.

8. *Donald's Dilemma* parodies the field of psychoanalysis.

9. Donald uses rubber cement in the waffle batter instead of baking soda.

10. In *Donald's Crime,* Donald robs his nephew's piggy bank in order to take Daisy out on a date.

11. Donald is lost in daydreams of horror and violence in this film.

12. Donald loses his lunch to ants in *Tea for Two Hundred* (1948).

13. Donald's nephews are Huey, Dewey, and Louie.

14. The darling nephews first appear in a film called, surprisingly enough, *Donald's Nephews* (1938).

15. In the "Lake of Titicaca" sequence, Donald tours Peru.

16. José Carioca is a singing, dancing, joking parrot.

17. Donald's farmer character is called Old MacDonald Duck.

18. The sequence from *Melody Time* featuring Donald and José is called "Blame it on the Samba."

19. The Three Caballeros are Donald Duck, José Carioca, and a brightly colored rooster called Panchito.

20. Donald falls for Aurora Miranda, Carmen Molina, and Dora Luz.

GOOFY

1. Goofy's first film is *Mickey's Revue* (1932.)

2. Goofy helps Mickey in the kitchen in *The Whoopee Party* (1932).

3. In *Mickey's Service Station,* Goofy serves as an auto mechanic.

4. Goofy attempts to catch fish by using chewing tobacco as bait. He waits for the fish to surface so they can spit out the tobacco and then he clubs them over the head.

5. Goofy has an absolutely awful time trying to load an upright piano onto the truck.

6. Goofy gets to be the front half of the moose decoy in *Moose Hunters*.

7. Goofy and Donald use a perfume called Deer Kiss to attract the hopefully amorous moose.

8. Wilbur is Goofy's pet grasshopper. He appears only in this film.

9. Goofy has a live decoy duck named Clementine in this film.

10. "How to Ride a Horse" is from the Disney feature *The Reluctant Dragon* (1941).

11. Goofy's horse's name is Percy.

12. Goofy is referred to as *Motoramus figitus, Neglecterus maximus, Driverius timidicus,* and *Stupidicus ultimus.*

13. Goofy's basketball film is called *Double Dribble.*

14. In *A Knight for a Day,* Goofy appears as Princess Penelope.

15. Goofy's son's name is Goofy, Junior.

16. Goofy's wife's name is never given. She is known simply as Mrs. Goofy.

17. In *Mickey's Christmas Carol,* Goofy plays the role of Marley's ghost.

18. Goofy was originally called Dippy Dawg in the comic strips.

19. Goofy walks on a ledge in *Clock Cleaners* (1937).

20. Goofy's film on hockey is titled *Hockey Homicide* (1945).

PLUTO

1. Pluto makes his first film appearance in *The Chain Gang* (1930).

2. In Pluto's second film, *The Picnic,* he goes by Rover.

3. Pluto belongs to Minnie Mouse in *The Picnic.*

4. There is a kitten, which goes on to take over Mickey's house, in the bag Pluto pulls from the river.

5. Mickey's goldfish is named Bianca.

6. The jury that is set to sentence Pluto is made up of cats, cats, and more cats.

7. Pluto ruins a performance by Donald Duck and Clara Cluck.

8. Pluto attempts to steal from the cage of a ferocious lion.

9. The Pluto film that features all those coyotes is called *The Coyote's Lament.* It was made in 1961. (This was a 1961 TV show; never released theatrically in the U.S.)

10. Pluto's heartthrob in *Pluto's Heartthrob* is Dinah, a dachshund.

11. *The Moose Hunt* (1931) is the first film in which Pluto is called Pluto.

12. The name of this golf film short is *Canine Caddy*.

13. Donald Duck is miserable to Pluto in *On Ice.*

14. Pluto's first great love is Fifi, a trouble-causing little brown dog.

15. Pluto is driven to the brink of sanity on more than one occasion by a kitten named Figaro.

ANSWERS
DISNEY
FEATURE
FILMS

TREASURE ISLAND

1. This Disney classic was based on a book by Robert Louis Stevenson.

2. The film opens in England in 1765.

3. The inn is called the Admiral Benbow Inn.

4. The man looking for Captain Billy Bones is called Black Dog.

5. Jim Hawkins is the young boy whose mother runs the inn.

6. After the boy tells Black Dog that Captain Bones isn't there, Black Dog sees the captain's foot locker hidden behind a drape.

7. In this first scene, the characters drink rum, as almost everybody does throughout the film.

8. The captain is given "the black spot" by a blind man. This symbolizes that he will be killed by those who sent it before very long.

9. Captain Bones entrusts Jim with a treasure map. It shows where Flint's gold is buried. (Flint has been a notorious pirate, and it is well known that he has quite a bit of gold stashed away somewhere.)

10. Jim returns with Squire Trelawney and Doctor Livesey to aid the captain.

11. The ship is called *The Hispaniola.*

12. Long John Silver is hired as the sea cook for the voyage. (What a mistake!)

13. Captain Smollett is chosen to command the crew on this voyage.

14. The first mate is Mr. Arrow, and he is disposed of by Long John Silver.

15. The penalty for carrying a concealed weapon aboard the ship is twelve lashes.

16. Jim is forced to hide in a barrel as the pirates enter the room, and he overhears their plot for mutiny.

17. The pirates take Jim Hawkins as a hostage and say they will trade him for the treasure map.

18. Ben Gunn is his name. He has been marooned for five years.

19. After the mutiny is successful, the pirates take down the British flag and raise the infamous "skull and crossed bones."

20. Long John Silver tells us, and the doctor concurs, that an apple a day will keep scurvy away.

21. Long John Silver tells Israel Hand and Haggott to stay behind and watch the ship. He also warns them not to drink too much rum.

22. Before he escapes to the island, he switches the flags back, raising the British flag once again.

23. The pirate crew gives their leader the dreaded "black spot."

24. The treasure has already been dug up by Ben Gunn. He has the bounty in his cave.

25. Long John Silver wants to give up his parrot, Captain Flint, to Jim.

20,000 LEAGUES UNDER THE SEA

1. The novel *20,000 Leagues Under the Sea* was written by Jules Verne.

2. The film takes place in 1868.

3. The first ship destroyed is the *Golden Arrow*.

4. Captain Nemo is the brains behind the *Nautilus*. He is played by James Mason.

5. Kirk Douglas plays the role of Ned Land, a master harpoonist.

6. The so-called Sea Monster is being pursued by Professor Pierre Aronnax.

7. Conseil was played by Peter Lorre.

8. The song is called "A Whale of a Tale."

9. The professor is a member of the Paris National Museum. He is on his way to the Orient.

10. The film won two Academy Awards: Best Visual Effects; and Best Art Direction, Set Direction.

11. The cream is actually milk from the giant sperm whale, and the pudding is a sauté of unborn octopus.

12. He serves them filet of sea snake and brisket of blowfish.

13. They are partaking in an underwater funeral.

14. The seal's name is Esmerelda.

15. Nemo's cigars are made of seaweed.

16. They do their farming at an underwater island called Crespo.

17. The *Nautilus* was built by Nemo himself at a place called Vulcania.

18. The only vital spot, according to Nemo, is directly between the eyes.

19. Captain Nemo is saved by Ned Land.

20. Captain Nemo is shot and dies aboard the *Nautilus*. Ironically, this takes place at Volcania, the place where Nemo's dream first took shape.

OLD YELLER

1. Old Yeller is set in the State of Texas.

2. Jim Coates is played by Fess Parker, of *Davy Crockett* fame. He is missing for most of the film because he is on a cattle drive.

3. Katie is played by Dorothy McGuire.

4. Old Yeller is seen chasing the Coateses' mule through the fields, destroying a great deal of the Coateses' property.

5. The Coateses' children are Travis and Arliss.

6. Travis had a dog named Old Bell when he was younger.

7. The mule's name is Jumper.

8. He hangs a piece of venison low to the ground, knowing that if Yeller takes it he will be justified in shooting him.

9. Arliss is wrestling with a bear cub and its mother begins to charge him. Yeller fights the bear off.

10. Bud Searcy, who is no help to anyone, is left behind to "protect" family and property.

11. Lisbeth knows that Yeller has been stealing bread, meat, and eggs from ranches in the area.

12. Travis gives Lisbeth a Comanche arrowhead.

13. Raccoons have been ruining the crop, so Travis and Yeller sleep in the patch to scare them off for good.

14. The cow that gives birth is named Rose.

15. Burn Sanderson is played by Chuck Connors.

16. Burn "trades" Yeller for Arliss's horny toad and a home-cooked meal.

17. Burn tells Travis that hydrophobia (rabies) is running rampant.

18. Travis and Yeller are attacked by wild hogs.

19. Katie stitches Yeller's wound with a needle and a hair from Jumper's (the mule) tail.

20. Yeller has been bitten by a diseased wolf and is slowly going mad.

21. Jim brings Katie a "store-bought" dress and a pair of shoes.

22. Jim brings Arliss an Indian headdress and toma-hawk. He brings Travis a horse.

POLLYANNA

1. *Pollyanna* was written by Eleanor H. Porter.

2. Nancy's boyfriend is George Dodds.

3. Mr. Thomas is the gardener.

4. Pollyanna's father was a minister.

5. Dinner time is at six for Aunt Polly.

6. Pollyanna's favorite game is the "Glad" game.

7. Pollyanna comes to live with her aunt when her father dies.

8. Angelica is the upstairs maid.

9. Aunt Polly buys new clothes for Pollyanna because her old ones came from a missionary barrel.

10. Whittier is Pollyanna's last name.

11. Dr. Edmund Chilton is the doctor who comes back to Harrington after many years away.

12. The reverend of the local church is Reverend Paul Ford.

13. Karl is the mayor's first name.

14. Death comes unexpectedly.

15. Jimmy Bean is Pollyanna's best friend.

16. Agnes Moorehead played Mrs. Snow.

17. Mrs. Snow's daughter's name is Millie.

18. The profits are to be used for a new orphanage.

19. Mrs. Snow makes a quilt.

20. God has told us to be glad 800 times.

21. Reverend Ford counts 826 happy texts in the Bible.

22. Pollyanna's favorite dessert is ice cream.

23. She falls from the tree and her legs become paralyzed.

24. She receives a doll at the bazaar's fishing pond.

25. Pollyanna goes to Baltimore for an operation.

26. Mr. Pendergast adopts Jimmy Bean.

27. Pollyanna gives the residents gladness.

28. The sign at the train station now reads: "Harrington—The Glad Town."

29. The water pipes burst at the orphanage.

30. Pollyanna is fascinated by the rainbows made by crystal prisms in Mr. Pendergast's home.

THE ABSENT MINDED PROFESSOR

1. Fred MacMurray played the role of the absent minded professor.

2. The professor's real name is Ned Brainard.

3. The professor teaches at Medfield College of Technology.

4. The professor teaches physical chemistry.

5. Professor Brainard is seen explaining the principle of acoustical energy.

6. Betsy Carlisle is supposed to become the professor's wife.

7. Professor Shelby Ashton (a romance-language professor at rival Rutland College) wants to steal Betsy from Professor Brainard.

8. The professor has already missed his wedding to Miss Carlisle two times previously.

9. The professor's housekeeper is Mrs. Chatsworth.

10. The professor's dog is Charlie.

11. There is an explosion in his garage-laboratory and he is, in fact, unconscious at the time he was to have wed.

12. The professor discovers flying rubber or "flubber," as he names it.

13. Alonzo Hawk, president of the Auld Lang Syne Co., wants to construct a housing tract on the college's property.

14. The president of Medfield College of Technology is Mr. Daggett.

15. The professor uses "flubber" to make his old Model-T not only run, but fly.

16. The "flubber," which allows the Medfield team members to jump to unbelievable heights, helps them beat Rutland 47–46.

17. Alonzo Hawk and his son Biff (a Medfield student) sight the professor flying his car.

18. They switch cars on the professor.

19. The students call the absent minded professor "Neddie the Nut."

20. He talks to J. Turnbull, special assistant to the President.

21. The professor walks into a harp while trying to recover his car from the Auld Lang Syne warehouse.

22. The fire chief is played by the fun-loving Ed Wynn.

THE PARENT TRAP

1. Sharon and Susan are played by Hayley Mills.

2. Mitch Evers is played by Brian Keith, and Margaret McKendrick by beautiful Maureen O'Hara.

3. The girls meet at Camp Inch.

4. The girls register with actress Nancy Kulp, otherwise known as Jane Hathaway in "The Beverly Hillbillies."

5. Sharon's roommates at summer camp are Betsy and Ursula.

6. The girls' bunkhouse is called Arapahoe.

7. The boy's camp participating in the coed dance is the Thunderhead Boys' Camp.

8. Sharon lives in Boston, Massachusetts, while Susan is a resident of Monterey, California.

9. The girls must bunk together for the remainder of the summer camp (four weeks).

10. Sharon shows Susan a picture of her mother and Susan recognizes the photo from having seen it at home.

11. Sharon and Susan were born on November 12.

12. Susan's dog is a German shephard named Andromeda.

13. The Everses' housekeeper is Verbena, and the ranch hand is Hecky.

14. After camp ends, the girls decide to switch places for a while.

15. Sharon has to start biting her nails.

16. Susan brings her grandmother a handmade birdcage made from popsicle sticks.

17. Mitch took Maggie to Martinelli's, an Italian restaurant in New York.

18. Vicky Robinson is played by actress Joanna Barnes.

19. It is pretty obvious that Vicky is after Mitch's money.

20. Mitch sometimes refers to Susan as "peanut face."

21. The girl's grandfather overhears a telephone conversation between Susan (in Boston) and Sharon (in California).

22. Susan wants her mother to compete with the younger woman her father is planning to wed, so they go to New York for some wardrobe updating and general "youthing" procedures.

23. Reverend Mosby (Leo G. Carroll) will be marrying Mitch and Vicky.

24. Verbena prepares veal parmigiana to do her part in reuniting the girl's parents.

25. Sharon and Susan perform a song called "Let's Get Together," which was an actual single later recorded by Hayley Mills.

26. They refuse to tell their parents their true identities, unless they promise to go on a three-day camping trip.

27. The girls plant a tree lizard on a canteen to frighten Vicky.

28. Two darling bear cubs are more than happy to remove the honey from Vicky's feet.

29. The group (except for Vicky) enjoys freshly caught trout for dinner.

30. The girls are the bridesmaids at the wedding of their parents, whom they have been successful in reuniting—the parent trap worked!

BABES IN TOYLAND

1. Victor Herbert and Glenn McDonough wrote the operetta *Babes in Toyland*.

2. Jack Donohue directed it.

3. Sylvester is a talking goose.

4. Tom and Mary's wedding takes place at Mother Goose Village.

5. Little Bo Peep is played by Ann Jillian.

6. Tom and Mary are played by Tommy Sands and Annette Funicello, respectively.

7. Lemonade is served.

8. Barnaby was played by Ray Bolger.

9. The toy maker was played by Ed Wynn.

10. Barnaby plans on kidnapping Tom.

11. Barnaby plans to throw Tom's body in the sea.

12. Mary wears a blue ribbon that night.

13. The glass on Mary's front door is heart-shaped.

14. Mary's last name is Contrary.

15. Little Bo Peep's sheep got lost in the Forest of No Return.

16. Toyland is closed for alterations.

17. The trees in the Forest of No Return are talking trees.

18. The toy maker's assistant is played by Tommy Kirk.

19. The toy machine explodes at half past October.

20. The first item shrunk by the toy maker is a chair.

21. The toy maker is the Mayor of Toyland.

22. When the wooden soldiers attacked Barnaby, Tom rides a yellow rocking horse.

23. Mary shoots Barnaby with a cannon boat.

24. Mary wears a red cape with fur trim on her wedding day.

25. Snowy.

MARY POPPINS

1. P. L. Travers wrote *Mary Poppins*.

2. The Bankses live on Cherry Tree Lane.

3. The number on the front door of the Bankses' home is 17.

4. Mrs. Brill is the cook, and Ellen is the housemaid.

5. The house shaped like a ship belongs to Admiral Boom.

6. George Banks has two children; their names are Jane and Michael.

7. Admiral Boom fires his cannon at eight o'clock in the morning.

8. Mary Poppins carries an umbrella and carpetbag.

9. Mary and the children meet Bert.

10. A spoonful of sugar helps the medicine go down.

11. Mary and Bert are served by penguin waiters.

12. Uncle Albert suffers from excessive laughter.

13. The tea party is held on Uncle Albert's ceiling.

14. The song is "Fidelity Fiduciary Bank" Mr. Banks takes his children to "Fidelity Fiduciary Bank."

15. The bird woman sells crumbs on the steps of St. Paul's Cathedral.

16. Mr. Dawes Sr. is chairman of the British bank.

17. Dick Van Dyke plays Bert and Mr. Dawes, Sr.

18. The Oscar-winning song "Chim-Chim-Cheree."

19. Bert draws chalk pictures on the sidewalks.

20. *Supercalifragilisticexpialidocious* is the only word to use when nothing else will do.

21. She refers to the wind.

22. Bert is the only person to see Mary Poppins fly away.

23. Mary Poppins's umbrella is unique because the tip has a talking-parrot head.

24. Mary Poppins favorite flavor is raspberry.

25. George Banks's wife's name is Winifred.

THE GNOME-MOBILE

1. Walter Brennan played D. J. Mulrooney and Knobby, a 943-year-old gnome.

2. *The Gnome-Mobile* song was written by Robert B. Sherman and Richard M. Sherman.

3. The gnomes live in a California Redwood Forest.

4. He thinks he's the last of the gnomes, and will never find a bride.

5. Jasper first speaks to Elizabeth, D. J. Mulrooney's granddaughter.

6. Gnomes call humans Do Deens.

7. The gnome-mobile is really a Rolls-Royce.

8. Horatio Quaxton kidnaps the gnomes.

9. They are kidnapped from the Cedar Creek Lodge to be used in Quaxton's Academy of Fantastic Freaks Show.

10. Knobby feels that lumbermen are ruining the forest—especially D. J. Mulrooney!

11. The head of security is Ralph Yarby, played by Richard Deacon.

12. Quaxton's mountain cabin is located on Old Willow Road.

13. The gnome mobile needs a lube job.

14. He is brought to a psychiatric center (sanitarium).

15. Rodney and Elizabeth help their grandfather escape.

16. The guard dog's name is Duke.

17. Rufus was played by Ed Wynn.

18. According to the "gnome law," the female gnome gets to choose her mate in a "Sadie-Hawkins" type race. If she can hold onto him for seven seconds, she can marry him.

19. Violet becomes Jasper's wife.

20. Their wedding present from D. J. is fifty thousand acres of virgin redwood.

THE HAPPIEST MILLIONAIRE

1. Richard M. Sherman and Robert B. Sherman wrote the music and lyrics.

2. Bill Thomas designed the costumes.

3. The film opens in 1916.

4. The Biddles live in Philadelphia.

5. Tommy Steele sings "Fortuosity."

6. Mrs. Duke lives in New York City.

7. John Lawless is played by Tommy Steele.

8. The employment agency that recommends Mr. Lawless is called Mayflower.

9. Mr. Lawless interviews for the butler's position.

10. Mrs. Worth was played by Hermione Baddeley.

11. Geraldine Page played Mrs. Duke.

12. Anthony is on a chocolate cake diet.

13. Biddle Bible Class is printed on the sweatshirts worn by Mr. Biddle and his daughter.

14. Mr. Biddle's daughter Cordelia is known as Cordy.

15. Mr. Biddle has two sons, named Tony and Livingston.

16. The pet alligator's name is George.

17. Cordy's brothers accidentally knock out Cordy's date.

18. Mr. Biddle feels Cordy has the best left hook.

19. He has twelve pet alligators that he captured in Florida.

20. The Wingfield School for Girls is located in Lakewood, New Jersey.

21. Rosemary is Cordy's roommate.

22. John Lawless comes from Ireland.

23. Walter Blakely and Robert Fitzsimmons are introduced to Cordy by Aunt Mary.

24. Cordy thinks the waltz is for old people until she dances with Angier Duke.

25. That U.S. President is Woodrow Wilson.

26. Aunt Mary and Mrs. Duke sing "There Are Those."

27. Gladys Cooper played Aunt Mary.

28. He offers them raisin tarts.

29. They go to Clancy's Bar.

30. They drink stout.

THE LOVE BUG

1. Jim Douglas is played by Disney veteran Dean Jones.

2. Carole Bennett is played by the lovely Michele Lee.

3. Buddy Hackett plays mechanic-eccentric Tennessee Steinmetz.

4. Jim crashes in car number 4B as the film opens.

5. Jim complains that Tennessee buys only parrot food. Tennessee defends his purchase by stating how healthy pressed kelp really is.

6. Tennessee traveled to Tibet to live and learn amid the gurus.

7. Jim is totally taken with the Thorndyke Special.

8. Herbie's license plate number is OFP 857.

9. Tennessee names Herbie after his uncle, the boxer.

10. Herbie drives Jim and Carole to a local drive-in burger joint.

11. The local "make-out" spot is Seabreeze Point.

12. Herbie races as number 53.

13. Herbie keeps spouting motor oil on Mr. Thorndyke.

14. Herbie sets a new qualifying time record at Laguna Seca.

15. Herbie sets a new track record at Tulare Fairgrounds.

16. Tennessee tells Mr. Thorndyke that his mother came from "Coney" Ireland.

17. Mr. Thorndyke pours Irish Coffee into Herbie's radiator.

18. Jim buys a red Lamborghini.

19. Herbie attempts to drive off the Golden Gate Bridge.

20. Mr. Wee becomes Herbie's new owner.

21. Thorndyke's partner is named Havershaw, as played by Joe Flynn.

22. The midpoint of the big race is Virginia City.

23. The number of the Thorndyke Special is 14.

BEDKNOBS AND BROOMSTICKS

1. *Bedknobs and Broomsticks* is set in England in 1940.

2. Eglantine Price is played by Angela Lansbury.

3. British army captain Greer is seen asking directions to Pepperinge Eye.

4. Because of the war, the museum is now used as a children's evacuation center.

5. Miss Price takes in Charles, Carrie, and Paul.

6. The package has been sent by Professor Emelius Browne (David Tomlinson), the curator of the College of Witchcraft in London.

7. The package contains a "flying" broomstick and a letter of congratulations on becoming an apprentice witch.

8. Miss Price drives a motorcycle with a sidecar, license plate C 41851.

9. Miss Price's cat is named Cosmic Creepers.

10. The spell is as follows:
    LAKIPO NIKRIF SCRUMPET LEETCH.

11. Miss Price turns Charles into a white rabbit. (She had threatened to turn him into a toad but couldn't quite pull it off.)

12. She entrusts the children with the "traveling spell." The spell is activated by tapping and turning a bedknob. You simply stated where you wished the bed to take you and it would be done.

13. The professor reneged on the last lesson in her witchcraft course and Miss Price is furious.

14. Professor Browne lives in an abandoned mansion at 8 Winfield Road.

15. The book is *The Spells of Astaroth*.

16. Half the book is missing and so is the spell she desperately desires.

17. Miss Price needs the spell on Substitutiary Locomotion (giving life to inanimate objects) to help the war effort.

18. Professor Browne is certain the book can be found on Portobello Road.

19. The wild animals, legend tells, settled on the isle of Naboombu.

20. The king of the isle of Naboombu is a lion.

21. He offers to referee a soccer game that was cancelled for lack of a referee. The king is the island's soccer star.

22. The king is wearing the medallion around his neck. (He never takes it off.)

23. The king plays soccer for the Dirty Yellows.

24. Two vultures eagerly wait on the sidelines for the next injury.

25. One has simply to say: TREGUNA MEKOIDES TRECORUM SATIS DEE.

26. The Nazi soldiers set up their headquarters at Miss Price's home.

27. The professor is waiting at the train station to go back to London.

28. Having been locked in a museum with hundreds of suits of armor and other war memorabilia, Miss Price uses her new spell to give these items life and they cause the Germans to retreat.

29. Before retreating, the Germans detonate explosives that destroy the wing of the house containing these items.

30. Professor Browne has enlisted and is marching off to war as the film closes.

ESCAPE TO WITCH MOUNTAIN

1. The children's names are Tony and Tia.

2. The children are transported to Pine Woods children's home.

3. Tony was five and Tia was three years old when they were adopted by the Malones.

4. Tia can "speak" to Tony without speaking at all—through mental telepathy.

5. The children warn Deranian to stay out of his car moments before it is demolished by a runaway truck.

6. The children of Pine Woods go to see Walt Disney's *Snow White and the Seven Dwarfs*.

7. Lucas Deranian is played by Donald Pleasence.

8. The children's black cat is named Winky.

9. Tia always carries her "star case," a small case with a double-star pattern on it.

10. After a plate has loosened, they find a map of Stony Creek under it.

11. Deranian has papers doctored to show him as their uncle and legal guardian.

12. Deranian works for Aristotle Bolt, who is played by Ray Milland.

13. The mansion is called Xanthus.

14. Bolt wants to use the children in assorted money and power-obtaining plots.

15. Bolt gives each of the children an ice cream cone (their favorite flavors are vanilla and strawberry).

16. Tia is instantly to tame the wild horse Thunderhead.

17. Tony needs to play the harmonica in order to put his powers into action.

18. Tia turns the tables—and the dogs—on their pursuers.

19. Jason O'Day is played by Eddie Albert.

20. Tia and Tony ask Jason to take them to Stony Creek, the place pictured on the map on Tia's star case.

21. First $1,000 is offered as a reward. After the children escape from jail, the ante is upped to $5,000, on the condition that they are captured alive.

22. The children are captured by the sheriff of Longview.

23. Jason's brother is Hiram O'Day.

24. Tony levitates a coat, hat, and broom, and it virtually attacks the sheriff as the children slip out.

25. Upon leaving the jail, Tia lets loose a caged bear and it follows the children for a short while.

26. They proclaim the children are witches from the mysterious Witch Mountain.

27. The population of Stony Creek is a meager 277.

28. They recall they were from another solar system and were rescued at sea when their spacecraft crash landed.

29. Uncle Bene, whom the children thought had died in the sea rescue, is played by Denver Pyle.

30. The children give Winky, their black cat, to Jason in the hopes he'll remember them. He assures them he will and asks if it would be all right if he remembered them as the children he never had.

THE APPLE DUMPLING GANG

1. *The Apple Dumpling Gang* is set in Quake City, California.

2. Quake City was built on the Calaveras Fault and was subject to earthquakes.

3. Sheriff Homer McCoy is played by Harry Morgan.

4. Sheriff McCoy is not only the sheriff, but the justice of the peace and the town barber.

5. Theodore Ogelvie is played by Don Knotts, and Amos Tucker by Tim Conway.

6. Ogelvie and Tucker call themselves The Hash-Knife Outfit.

7. They were members of the dreaded Stillwell Gang until Amos accidentally shot Frank Stillwell in the leg.

8. Amos Tucker's mule is named Clarise.

9. Susan Clark's character is Magnolia Dusty Clydesdale.

10. Magnolia rides for the Butterfly Stage and Freight Company. It is owned by T. R. Clydesdale, as played by David Wayne.

11. Russell Donavan is played by Bill Bixby.

12. The "valuables" are Bobby, Clovis, and Celia Bradley, three children.

13. John Wintle is the children's "second uncle or something," as described by Dusty Clydesdale.

14. The horse with the bad choppers is Diablo.

15. Dusty makes Sonofagun stew and brings the leftovers to the children for dinner.

16. Their father has left the Bradley children the Commodore Mine.

17. The Commodore Mine is located on Bold Hill.

18. A huge gold nugget weighing 356 pounds was knocked free by the quake.

19. Suddenly everyone wants to adopt the children, and get his hands on the nugget, worth nearly a million dollars.

20. The nugget is displayed at the Quake City Bank.

21. The local café is the Hard Times Café.

22. Sheriff McCoy charges "4 bits" for a shave.

23. Sheriff McCoy charged two dollars for a wedding ceremony.

24. They originally think it's their mine, but in fact the car is from the Moonridge Mine 2.

25. The two bumblers are sentenced to be hung by the big oak tree near Boot Hill at twelve o'clock sharp. (They are even told to bring their own rope.)

26. Frank Stillwell poses as a reverend.

27. Stillwell grabs Celia as he is escaping from the bank.

28. Stillwell and one of his partners in crime escape on the local fire wagon.

29. Russel Donavan gets $5,000 for capturing Frank Stillwell.

30. Clovis delivers a swift kick to the nearest shin of anyone who touches him.

PETE'S DRAGON

1. Miss Taylor is a schoolteacher.

2. Charlie Callas is the voice of Elliott.

3. Lampie is Nora's father and they live at the lighthouse by the sea.

4. The town Pete and Elliott visit is Passamaquoddy.

5. Jim Backus played the role of the Mayor.

6. Onna White was responsible for the choreography of the film.

7. Elliott eats apples.

8. Elliott makes a baked apple for Pete.

9. Nora gives Pete chowder upon his arrival.

10. Paul is Nora's fiancé.

11. Pete's two friends are Elliott and Nora.

12. Elliott sleeps in the caves near the lighthouse.

13. Jim Dale plays Dr. Terminus.

14. He says the medicines come from Paris.

15. The number on the lighthouse is 1879.

16. Lena's husband's name is Merle.

17. Pete catches a lobster.

18. The Gogans have a bill of sale.

19. Nora meets Elliott one stormy night at the light-house.

20. The Gogans paid $50 plus legal fees.

21. Nora gives Elliot a kiss.

22. There are no other survivors.

23. The ship went down in Cape Hatteras.

24. Hoagy is his name, as played by Red Buttons.

25. She says she'll be Paul's "Candle on the Water" (his lighthouse).

THE BLACK HOLE

1. Our cast begins their travels through space in a ship called the *Palomino*.

2. The commander of the *Palomino* is Captain Holland.

3. The hovering robot aboard the *Palomino* is named V.I.N.CENT

4. V.I.N.CENT's model number is L.F. 396.

5. The vessel that the crew of the *Palomino* comes across is the USS *Cygnus*.

6. The *Cygnus* is commanded by Captain Reinhardt, as played by actor Maximilian Schell.

7. Charlie Pizer (Joseph Bottoms) remains behind with the *Palomino* when the rest of the crew boards the *Cygnus*.

8. The *Cygnus* is positioned at the mouth of the black hole and is not moving at all.

9. Dr. Alex Durant is played by veteran actor Anthony Perkins.

10. Dr. Durant is killed by Reinhardt's "henchman" robot Max, who possesses rotary blades for hands and uses them to do in the doctor.

11. Kate McCrae is able to speak to V.I.N.CENT telepathically.

12. Kate's father was a crew member of Reinhardt's aboard the *Cygnus* and she wonders if, after all these years, presumed lost or dead, he could still be alive.

13. The robot V.I.N.CENT befriends aboard the *Cygnus* is named Old B.O.B.

14. V.I.N.CENT challenges S.T.A.R. to a laser shootout after he humiliates his pal Old B.O.B.

15. Reinhardt serves mushroom soup to his dinner guests.

16. The crew has been turned into humanoids by Reinhardt. They obey his every command and have no minds of their own.

17. Harry Booth (as played by Ernest Borgnine) attempts to save himself by escaping in the *Palomino*.

18. The remaining members of the crew attempt to escape the *Cygnus* aboard its probe ship.

19. The probe ship has been programmed to travel into the black hole, and it does.

20. Reinhardt is killed by falling debris during a "structural overload" aboard the *Cygnus*.

ANSWERS
DISNEY'S
THEME
PARKS

DISNEYLAND

1. Disneyland opened on July 17, 1955.

2. Fantasyland is dedicated to the young and the young at heart; to those who believe that when you wish upon a star, your dreams do come true.

3. The letters given were A–E (A—least expensive; E—most expensive).

4. His apartment was located on Main Street over the fire house.

5. The biggest flop in Disneyland was The Mickey Mouse Club Circus.

6. The *Mark Twain* rules as "Queen of the River."

7. Disneyland's first "thrill ride" was the Matterhorn.

8. Former President Richard M. Nixon was on hand with his family for the monorail dedication.

9. On that day, the "pilot" was Art Linkletter.

10. Soviet Premier Nikita Khrushchev was unable to get into Disneyland because the local government officials were not convinced that enough security precautions could be taken at the park.

11. This tree is located in Frontierland.

12. Disney people called it *Disneyodendron semperflorens grandis,* which means, "large, ever-blooming Disney tree."

13. It's a Small World opened at Disneyland in 1966.

14. The pirates sing "Yo Ho (A Pirate's Life for Me)."

15. The town is called Rainbow Ridge.

16. Captain EO is played by singer Michael Jackson.

17. Captain EO was produced by George Lucas and directed by Francis Ford Coppola.

18. The base of the flagpole was picked up on Wilshire Boulevard at the scene of a traffic accident.

19. The base was bought for $5.00.

20. The horses are Percherons, Belgians, and Clydesdales.

WALT DISNEY WORLD

1. Walt Disney World opened to the public on October 1, 1971.

2. Marty and Bill Windsor, Jr., from Lakeland, Florida, and their sons, Jay and Lee, were the first family to enter the Magic Kingdom.

3. Upon entering the Kingdom you are on Main Street.

4. The four steam engines are "Walter E. Disney," "Lilly Belle," "Roger E. Broggie," and "Roy O. Disney."

5. We are referring to the Main Street Electrical Parade.

6. It is called topiary gardening.

7. The tallest structure in Walt Disney World is Cinderella Castle, which is more than 180 feet high.

8. The restaurant is called King Stefan's Banquet Hall.

9. "Fantasyland" is known as "The Happiest Kingdom of Them All."

10. a. "Snow White's Adventures"
    b. "Peter Pan's Flight"
    c. "Mr. Toad's Wild Ride"

11. There are 90 horses.

12. There are 12 submarines, each with a 38-seat capacity.

13. The Jungle Cruise was inspired by Disney's "True-Life Adventures."

14. The feeling was that Florida was close enough to the real location. Pressure from guests who had seen it at Disneyland, however, caused it to be built.

15. The storyline tells of a capture and the ultimate burning of a seacoast town by a crew of pirates.

16. We are referring to Frontierland's hottest attraction, Big Thunder Mountain.

17. Grizzly Hall is home to the Country Bear Jamboree.

18. There are 17 bears. Big Al and Swingin' Teddi Barra are two of the most popular stars.

19. The Liberty Oak Tree is approximately 40 feet tall, 60 feet wide, and weighs more than 38 tons.

20. In the Hall of Presidents, Abraham Lincoln speaks for all the Presidents.

21. There are 999 ghosts who occupy the Haunted Mansion.

22. Space Mountain came on the scene in 1975, after ten years in development.

23. Space Mountain towers nearly 175 feet above the ground.

24. DACS controls and monitors all aspects of show performances "onstage" throughout Walt Disney World, from the opening and closing of theater doors to the singing of bears and birds and the speeches of pirates and Presidents.

25. The Walt Disney World trash-disposal system is called AVAC—Automated Vacuum Assisted Collection.

26. We are talking about the beautiful Contemporary Resort Hotel.

27. The enormous open area of this hotel is called the Grand Canyon Concourse.

28. The uppermost floor of this hotel is referred to simply as the Top of the World.

29. The monorail system is called The Walt Disney World Mark IV Monorail System.

30. The aquatic highway we are referring to is called the Seven Seas Lagoon.

1. EPCOT stands for Experimental Prototype Community of Tomorrow.

2. The sphere is called Spaceship Earth, and it is 180 feet high.

3. The sponsor of Spaceship Earth is the Bell System. The Universe of Energy is sponsored by Exxon.

4. As we ride through the Universe of Energy, we come face to face with prehistoric reptiles.

5. The World of Motion building is shaped like a wheel.

6. The robot's name is Tiger.

7. The World of Imagination is hosted by Dreamfinder and Figment.

8. The largest of all the EPCOT pavilions is The Land.

9. This nutrition show is called "Kitchen Kabaret."

10. Communicore is short for "community core," which is designed to take the mystery out of technology.

11. a. Energy Exchange—Exxon
    b. Future Com—Bell System
    c. TravelPort—American Express

12. The American Adventure's hosts are Mark Twain and Benjamin Franklin.

13. The American Adventure ends on the platform beneath the torch flame of the Statue of Liberty.

14. The two major areas of EPCOT Center are:
    1. Future World
    2. World Showcase

CLOSING

The Beatles once wrote a song called "Magical Mystery Tour." They might have been referring to the marvelous, mystical journey we take every time we involve ourselves with a Disney production. Every time we turn on the TV Sunday night to witness Tinker Bell spreading that dust, there is magic in our hearts— magic that keeps us waiting in line with our own children to see one of Disney's rereleased classics, magic that soars whenever we cross into an enchanted Disney kingdom.

Disney magic represents the American dream at its fullest. The stories and characters of Walt Disney's enterprise know no bounds of language, culture, or politics. We bless the hope they inspire in all of us, the sense of renewal they bring.

If our trivia tribute leaves you with anything, let it be Disney's own legacy: When you wish upon a star—if you truly believe—your dreams can come true.